Rearrange It!

How to Start a Profitable Interior Redesign Business

or

How to Generate Wealth and Financial Freedom with a One-Day Decorating Business

Barbara Jennings, CRS/CSS

Table of Contents

Chapter One - 5
Introduction – Benefits to Expect – About the Author – Need for Design Training

Chapter Two - 23
What It Takes – What a Re-designer Does – Effective Communication – Being Service Oriented – Knowledge of Interior Design – Personal Attitudes – Professional Image – Professional Ethics – Entrepreneurial Skills - Finding Your Niche – Clients Who Suit You - Travel Distances

Chapter Three - 32
Defining a Need – Why Homeowners Need Help – Working with Decision Makers – What Homeowners Need Most

Chapter Four - 35
Generating Leads – Satisfied Clients – Centers of Influence – Scouts and Leads Clubs – Yellow Pages – Websites – Personal Observations – New Buyers Lists – Moving Companies – Home Staging Services - Other Methods

Chapter Five - 44
Getting Appointments – Making Contact – Prospects Contacting You – Direct Mail – Business Cards – Phone Discussions – Styles and Color Palette – Taking Accessories

Chapter Six - 52
Consultant Etiquette – Tools of the Trade – First Impressions – Gaining Control – Doing a Walk Thru – Initial Interview – Choosing the Room – Starter Questions – Give and Take Process – Waiver Form – Payment Agreement – Before Pictures – Taking Measurements – Traffic Patterns

Chapter Seven - 65
Assessing the Room – Main Seating Arrangement – Secondary Arrangements – Other Furniture – Placing Accessories – Handling Possessions –Advising on Style –Goals of Design – Client Feedback – Collecting Fee – Referrals – Testimonials – After Pictures – New Purchases – Leaving Cards – Thank You Notes – Reminders

Chapter Eight - 79
Charging for Services – The Right Fee – Quoting Fees – Other Expenses - Your Guarantee

Chapter Nine - 84
Managing Your Business – Legal Structures – Selecting Business Name – Business Licenses – Payroll – Mission Statement – Business Plan – Start Up Budget – Creating Invoices – Bank Accounts – Business Telephone – Business Address, Marketing Materials – Automobile – Tax Preparation

Chapter Ten - 96
Publicity and Advertising – Press Releases – Creating News – Advertising –Word of Mouth – Directory Listings

Chapter Eleven - 102
Strategies for Success – Economic Climate – Continuing Education – The Savings Rule – Strategy of Preeminence

Chapter Twelve - 107
Marketing Interview - Sample Design Plan - Getting People to Call You –Generating Referrals –Reaching Niche Market

Chapter Thirteen - 119
The Power of One – Case Study –Developing a Marketing Plan - Staying Organized – Getting Complimentary Publicity

Chapter Fourteen - 128
Becoming a Strategic Force in the Industry

Chapter Fifteen - 137
The Secret Art of Hanging Art

Chapter Sixteen - 155
Common Furniture Arrangements That Work

Chapter Seventeen - 167
Additional Resources – Testimonials

Chapter One

Introduction

BEFORE REDESIGN

I've been professionally rearranging the homes of clients since 1986 in Southern California. I am the West Coast pioneer in the concept of redecorating any client's room instantly by simply rearranging their current furnishings and accessories using the same concepts professional designers and decorators have used for decades. The photo above is an example of one such client's living room. This is how it looked when I arrived. Next is the same room, using the same furniture in the room or brought in from other rooms and how it looked when the re-design was finished.

AFTER REDESIGN - It has long been my desire to help my clients, not only to achieve a beautiful interior that is comfortable and functional, but to teach them in the process, so that in the future they can make adjustments or simply change the way their home looks from time to time. My own home gets constant adjustments. This is probably the way it is for most creative people. We get bored easily and are constantly looking for a new creative challenge. If you're the same way, then the business of redesign is perfect for you.

I don't know why it is, but every time I have guests, I wind up rearranging everything within days after my guests leave. I don't know, maybe I have some secret desire to remain "mysterious" and need to change things immediately after someone has seen that part of my personality. Because, you see, design is an expression of your personality.

BEFORE REDESIGN - When you design the interiors belonging to other people, you need to be able to capture their personality (not yours). Otherwise they will not keep the arrangement you create for them. They will not feel comfortable with it. Sometimes if drastic changes are made when you are rearranging, it will take some time for them to become adjusted to the "new look", just like getting a new haircut that is very different from what they had in the past.

This client suffered the loss of a 16 year-old daughter from cancer. Subsequent to that she and her husband divorced and she moved into a new residence. But she was at a loss as to

how to make the home feel and look comfortable, and she wanted to keep precious memories of her daughter around, especially in the living room over the fireplace. As I worked with this client, and cried with her as she related her story, it was my pleasure to work on her behalf to accomplish all of the dreams and goals she had for her home and her remembrances of her daughter.

AFTER REDESIGN - By rearranging her furniture and all of the accessories, not only for this room, but for several other rooms, we were able to achieve all she wanted. She was thrilled with the outcome.

The closer you, as a professional, can come to making someone instantly "love" what you did for them, the longer they will keep the arrangement and appreciate what you have done. Only then will they feel comfortable recommending your services to their family, friends and acquaintances.

You see, a lot of people don't know how to properly arrange their furniture and accessories. The mistakes they make are very common. But everyone knows what they like *when they see it.* So you need to listen very carefully during the interview portion you will learn to do. You'll need to ask the right questions and then try to utilize all that information when you plan out the new arrangement.

One of my senior citizen clients told me at the end of her consultation, "I asked you to come just to see what you would do. But I thought I had really done a great job of arranging things myself. So after you did your rearrangement, I had really planned on changing everything back to the way it was before. But I can't believe how much better it looks the way you've done it, so I'm going to keep it. You did things I never would have thought to do."

Now that's the perfect response and should be the goal of every re-design consultant.

Benefits You Can Reasonably Expect

I don't know about you, but I love a business idea that has minimal overhead and minimal risk. That couldn't be truer of the home rearrangement consulting business. You are providing a service and not a product. That means there is nothing to inventory. Nothing to send out. You get paid instantly upon completion of the service. The costs to generate business and maintain it are quite low.

You can do it part time or full time. You can work from your home. You work strictly by appointment, so you have the luxury of working when you want to. You can have another career at the same time. You can work around your family as needed.

The career is fresh and innovative. It's prestigious. It's very creative and challenging and no two projects are ever alike. You have no boss except yourself. You can choose your clients and don't have to work for any prospects that make you feel uncomfortable.

You can work as much as you want or as little as you want. What more do you want?

You can also learn how to simultaneously offer a home staging business. I cover this business thoroughly in my basic business tutorial called, *Home Staging for Profit*. Please see the last chapter of this book for details on this book, my courses, and all of the sales aids and other tools of the trade that I have developed to help you become as successful as you work to become. I encourage you to add home staging to your services because it will help you build your redesign business and vice versa.

If you should decide you would like to take a complete course, we will give you full credit for the purchase of this manual if you purchased it directly from us (not including shipping/handling). If you purchased this training elsewhere, we will gladly make substitutions of equal value. You must call us or write us first and we will tell you what credit or substitution you qualify to receive.

Complimentary Newsletter Available

To receive the complimentary design newsletter that is issued twice a month, request your copy by writing to: **support4@barbarajennings.com**.

A Little Bit About Me

I am a Southern California interior re-designer plus a home stager, an artist, author and consultant. My career in design began in 1972 when I began my own graphic arts and printing business. Over the next eleven years, I was responsible for the design and production of thousands of pieces of printed material, including books, newsletters, newspapers, brochures, flyers, catalogs, TV and Radio Guides, letterhead, and a wide variety of other 2-dimensional pieces of media.

In 1983, having tired of the graphic arts business, I began a successful corporate art consulting career of my own. I have designed and implemented hundreds of art collections for small, medium, and large businesses, including several Fortune 1000 and Fortune 500 companies. During that time, I wrote and self published the popular book of 101 wall grouping designs called, "Where There's a Wall -- There's a Way" (republished and improved under the title "Wall Groupings!").

It was also at this time that I returned to college to study art. I had been selling and showing the work of other artists for many years, and now I wanted to see if I could successfully create and market my own images.

Simultaneously, in 1986, while marketing my book on wall groupings, I began to market my redesign and staging services. Up until that time, traditional design was merely thought of as a "rich person's" luxury. Interior designers urged people to toss out the old furnishings and begin from scratch. They made their profits on re-doing everything virtually so it usually left average folks without professional help.

My concept was simply to work with clients on a smaller scale. I had discovered by that time that the average American homeowner has a pretty good sense of what furnishings and accessories to acquire, but where they struggle most is in the area of furniture and accessory **placement**. Without good placement, the most beautiful furnishings don't live up to expectations and the rooms look unsettling, to put it as simply as I can.

Unknowingly, another designer across the nation from me had discovered the same realizations though we did not know each other. Today the concepts of redesign (and home staging) are widely known and are growing services being offered to consumers. You are starting your business at an opportune time. The concept is still relatively new enough that you're not likely to have much competition in your area, yet it has received enough publicity to now be recognized as a very legitimate option to traditional high end interior design.

Since 1986, I have simultaneously served both corporate and residential clients with art and redesign and staging services respectively. In addition to that, I have become a published artist and author. I have numerous corporate collectors and my work has been published in the form of prints by The McGaw Group of New York and Galaxy of Graphics of New York.

Our current websites are: Decorate-Redecorate.Com, HomeStaging4Profit.Com, ArrangingFurniture.Com and WorkingWomen911.Com.

The Need for Furniture Arrangement Training is Essential

If you don't have a degree in interior design already, I strongly urge you to get the proper design training in the areas of furniture and accessory arrangement. It's one thing to decorate for your self. It's another thing to decorate for a friend or relative for free. But it's a whole other ball game to decorate for a stranger for a fee. They will ask a lot of questions. You need to be able to answer their questions intelligently and confidently. You also need to be totally confident and know that you can handle any situation. You'll be able to do that if you know the professional concepts, techniques and methods professionals use.

You need to get the instruction, the proper instruction, if you want to succeed. Clients

expect to see real changes, significant changes, when they are paying you to solve their problems. Simple differences aren't going to cut it. See the last chapter for plenty of resources for training beyond the scope of this book.

TYPICAL **BEFORE** ROOM – Wouldn't you agree that this living room has some real problems that make it uninteresting and uninviting? To build a successful redesign consultation business you need to be good at what you do and extremely confident. You need to be able to walk into a room like this and know instantly what's wrong and how to fix it. You'll need to be able to study it on the spot and come up with a workable solution. That takes knowledge, talent and skill. You can't go home and look anything up. You can't ask a friend. You've got to solve the problem right there on the spot in the client's home. It can be a challenge. But it is also a whole lot of fun and very rewarding every time you succeed.

AFTER REDESIGN - JUST ONE OF MANY WAYS THIS ROOM COULD HAVE BEEN ARRANGED
By taking the furniture and accessories already in the room, combining it when necessary with furnishings from other parts of the home (even the garage or attic or basement), the room is "re-designed" using standard interior design principles and concepts. The results are often amazing and dramatic. Clients marvel at your creativity and wonder why they couldn't do it themselves.

www.decorate-redecorate.com

Other Aspects for Success

You need to be likeable too. While this manual will take you very far, it is not generally enough in and by itself to sustain you in a business like this, particularly if you've never owned a business before.

So I hope you will visit the website often and see all of the additional training and tools of the trade that we make available to you. Your success is our success. We're not interested in just getting you some basic information. We are interested in helping you long term to turn this knowledge into action and let your actions bring you monetary rewards, creativity and enjoyment.

It's not a matter of the client lacking the ability. It is a matter of the client's lack of training. Interior redesign is not difficult. I mean, it's not rocket science. It's common sense, actually. But you'd be literally amazed at the number of people who have no clue as to how to properly arrange their furniture and accessories.

Quite often clients have a multitude of family photographs or other memorabilia on shelf units. So you'll be called upon to organize it and arrange it in a way that is both attractive and enhances the client's treasures. Usually when you find shelf units or entertainment centers that have shelves you'll find a disorderly mess you have to completely rearrange. People do not know how to arrange their shelves and there will usually be a complete mish-mash of everything under the sun. You'll need to understand scale, proportion, balance and other design aspects to make the shelves as attractive as the rest of the room. You'll need to understand the usage of any room you re-design and make it as functional and enjoyable for your clients as you possibly can. The room should also look "lived in" and not so sterile that your clients feel uncomfortable.

As a re-designer you'll need to know some basic guidelines and "rules" for working with collectibles, photos, and other smaller accessories, not just furniture. It's a challenge sometimes – but oh so worth it. If you take the design training I also offer separately, you'll learn all about groupings – furniture groupings, wall groupings, shelf groupings and table groupings. When you know how to do groupings (vignettes), you'd be amazed how much you can display for a client and still keep the design beautiful and organized.

And just in the ordinary process of doing what you've been hired to do, you'll make some amazing friendships. You can't work for several hours in someone's home without getting to know them. Some clients want you to just do the work and not involve them. Then there are others that want you to teach them and they want to be part of the transformation process. As the day progresses you tend to bond with each other. This is important because your client has the ability to refer you to other people who have a need for your services. And that's an easy way to build your business.

BEFORE REDESIGN - You'll have a chance to work in all types of homes, from modestly priced homes of middle income clients, to multi-million dollar homes. Here is one such home of a very affluent client of mine. You can see that although the home is elegant and there is furniture in the living room, it lacks personality. You'll learn about the importance of accessories – for they carry the personality of the homeowner. But it's not just a matter of having accessories, but it's where they are placed in the room that is essential to completing the look properly. Put them in the wrong place and the whole design is ruined. Use too many and the room looks cluttered and you feel uneasy. Use too few and the room feels sparse and incomplete. A good re-designer develops a sixth sense about what is needed and looks to achieve just the right balance.

AFTER REDESIGN - A good re-designer understands the purposes of various accessories, what size and shape they should be, as well as what colors.

There are many aspects to good design: form, size, scale, proportion, texture, line, rhythm, color, balance, just to name a few elements.

Do you know what these terms mean? Do you know how to apply them to a given situation? Developing your business isn't just about letting people know you're in business. Yes, you've got to do that, and then some. But once you get the job, you've got to perform and turn that client's home into a beautiful space – no matter what the home looks like – no matter what the furnishings look like – no matter how old or dated everything is - no matter what you have to work with.

But don't worry. I've got you covered on any topic you feel you need more help. As you digest this manual, you'll hear me saying over and over again that you've got to get your design training as well. The more you know, the more confidence you will have. The more confidence you have, the better people will respond to you and your service.

You don't have to be certified by me or anyone else to be successful. But you do need to know what you're doing from a design stand point. There is a lot to cover. I can't do it in this manual because here we're focused strictly on the business side of starting, running and growing your business. So that's why I've broken it into segments. Everyone comes from different backgrounds, with different goals and different knowledge and experiences. No one manual can be all things to all people. Nor do all people need the same things. So I encourage you, as you work your way through this manual, to keep an open mind. See the opportunity that awaits you. Know in your heart that you can learn this business. Given time, if you learn what I'm about to teach you, and if you **apply** what you learn, you stand an excellent chance of realizing your dreams. You can do this business. You really can.

Anyone Can Do This Business Once Trained

You don't need a degree to do a redesign business. All over the country and around the globe, people just like you are starting their own interior redesign business.

They come from all types of backgrounds. Some were secretaries. Some were nurses. Some were accountants. Some were homemakers, teachers, stagers, real estate agents, cleaning ladies – you name it. They are all ages. All races. Male and female – though the greatest percentage are female.

You may feel a bit overwhelmed right now, but not to worry. You can do this business if you study the material, get your design training as it pertains to the arrangement of furniture and accessories, and proceed forward. Here are just four examples of my many students who have become highly successful.

BEFORE REDESIGN – Isn't this a typical high school student's bedroom? Posters all over the wall. Crowded. A bit messy. This homeowner's son got married and moved out. The room was to then be converted to a guest bedroom, but a lot of work needed to be done. So the re-designer went to work.

AFTER REDESIGN – The vertical blinds were covered over with some sheer drapes to soften the room yet allow plenty of light into the room. The walls were all painted white. The bed was kept in the same location as it was the only place where it could be placed. A bedspread was brought from the closet and put over the bed, which was also put on rollers to give the bed more height. A night stand and lamp were brought in from another room. A thin shelf was acquired for over the bed, as were some throw pillows. But essentially most of the room's furnishings were already owned by the homeowner – they just needed to be brought into the room for a completely different look.

Some of the changes in this room go beyond the scope of this manual as they include elements beyond the rearrangement of furniture and accessories. But that's the beauty of having your own business. You can involve yourself with window treatments, providing a shopping service for bedding, lamps, wall art, floral arrangements, paint and a wide variety of other products and services. It's totally up to you.

BEFORE REDESIGN – This client had moved into a new home and brought their furnishings from a previous residence, as is common in the industry. After living in the home for a while, she became restless with the way it was arranged. And no wonder because the arrangement was completely helter-skelter. None of the furniture faced or included the fireplace. The room was completely off balance and there was no cohesion. A TV was placed opposite where you see the sofa at this time, so you can see that it was completely out of position for the space. Not only would members of the family have to cross in front of anyone watching the TV, the seating arrangements were way too far away to make watching TV a pleasant experience. There is no conversation area and the art on the wall at the back is hung almost at the ceiling. (The client's husband was tall.)

AFTER REDESIGN – As you can see, the sofa was turned around and repositioned near the fireplace. The TV (which had been at the far end of the room opposite the fireplace) was brought close to the fireplace as well, against the wall. Now anyone can sit on the sectional and watch TV while enjoying a fire in the fireplace on a cold night. In this open floor plan, the repositioning of the sofa also helped to define the actual living room, separating it visually from the dining room, kitchen and entry. An intimate conversational area was created and better use of the floor space made the room more functional as well as more attractive. The mirror over the fireplace should have been lowered closer to the mantel as the gap between the base of the mirror and the mantel is too large, but at least there are some accessories there to help close the gap.

BEFORE REDESIGN – This master bedroom was in need of a major change with a rearrangement service. The bed was placed in front of the window on the left. A door in the corner to a self-made extra room over the kitchen made that corner of the room awkward and made it extremely difficult to balance the wall on the right as a result. The TV on the chest of drawers detracted from the look of the room and a singular eyesore. A large sofa table was placed at the foot of the bed. The good thing about the room was that it was large and there were plenty of furnishings to work with to bring about a successful transformation. So let's see what the end result looked like.

The client also wanted to change the color palette of the room. Plum was a hot decorating color at the time and it was one of her favorites. So the redesign was to involve more than just rearranging what was in the room. Purchases were going to have to be made to complete the whole look.

A plan of action was conceived and little by little it was achieved. You can provide a service to your client or just give them clear direction and turn them loose to shop for themselves. The latter is more risky, of course, as you never know what they're going to go buy, but many people prefer this route to save money and they're pretty good about following your directions if you give them direction on color, size and shape.

AFTER REDESIGN– The bed was flipped to the right side wall. Draperies were added to soften the room, add additional visual height and hide the unsightly door in the corner (which was not used all that often). New art was added over the bed, along with a new bedspread and decorative throw pillows. A desk the client had was placed in front of the window for practicality. The chest of drawers was moved to the shorter wall in the corner where the proportion is better. A chest was changed out at the foot of the bed in place of the sofa table that was placed there previously. The room not only is more visually appealing, it has greater drama and cohesion and the client was thrilled with the final outcome.

BEFORE AND AFTER REDESIGN - (next page) - Dark walls and considerable disorganization met this re-designer when she arrived at this client's home. But after assessing the room and correcting the decorating problems by toning down the colors and adding a window treatment, plus a new furniture arrangement, the re-designer changed the whole room and brought order out of chaos. Not all situations require a drastic change like this one. You can become as involved in a project as you want to be or feel competent to handle. If you do not feel confident, tell the client is it outside the scope of your service or recommend someone who can handle that part of the project for you.

Before

After

21 – Rearrange It! How to Start a Profitable Interior Redesign Business

When you work for payment, clients will ask you questions. You want your answers to be correct and authoritative and correct, so don't tackle areas you are not competent enough to handle on a professional level. Get help or move on.

The students who achieved some of these transformations have all completed the requirements for double certification in home staging and interior redesign through one of our Diamond courses. For information on our certification program, please visit the website or see the last chapter of this book. While certification is not mandatory for success, as more and more people enter the field who claim to be certified or "accredited" by other organizations, you will find it becoming increasingly important to attain a designation for yourself.

I am very proud of all my students who have worked hard to develop their talents and have gone on to build successful businesses of their own. The same story could be said about you as you apply what you learn and give your business time to grow and prosper.

About The Pictures in This Book

You're looking at real world, un-touched photographs taken immediately at the beginning and conclusion of actual recent redesign projects. These are the types of pictures you'll find yourself photographing for your portfolio (unless you are a professional photographer or you hire one). Don't be concerned. You never have to hire a professional photographer for your pictures to convey your talents well enough to prospective clients, either in person or on the web. Naturally yours will be in color. To keep publishing costs low for this small niche market, the publisher necessarily had to reproduce the photos in this book in black and white. But regardless of whether photos are in color or not, you should be able to see that the changes can be subtle or pretty dramatic. Every project is different. But in every case, the room's appearance has been improved and the clients were amazed and very happy.

Sometimes you will work in a new home with new furniture. Sometimes you will work in a new home with old furniture. Sometimes you will work in an old home with old furniture. Sometimes you will work in an old home with new furniture. None of this matters. You've been hired to make the room look fantastic whether the client's furnishings are old or new, whether they are stylish or not, whether they look great together or not, whether they are trendy or dated.

Don't be judgmental of what your client owns.

Don't make the mistake of judging these photos as "dated" either. **That is the nature of our business.** The photos are current, but the homes or furnishings very well may be dated. That's what makes it such a rewarding challenge. You will quickly discover that bringing professional arrangement skills to a room will transform it immediately into a charming space – I guarantee it – even if the furnishings leave a bit to be desired.

You will work with what is already there, and if you want, you might be able to make even more money by shopping on behalf of your client. But the beauty of the business is that you can get as involved as you want, or you can keep it quite simple and straightforward. It's your business. And each person decides for themselves how vested they become in any single project or service.

Chapter Two

What It Takes
Your Expertise

If you have a degree in interior design or have taken many classes in the subject, then you're already ahead of the game. But for those who have not, don't worry. You do not need a degree in interior design to be successful as an arrangement specialist.

What you do need, however, is some specific training in arrangement design so that you can walk in to any situation and feel confident and competent to improve the situation.

With that said, here is a brief list of the educational and business skills you should have (or be prepared to acquire) if you want to be good at your profession and gain the respect you will need to continue as a successful consultant and business person.

- a working knowledge of arrangement design that includes furniture and accessories
- a working knowledge of all other aspects of design, such as color, carpeting, wall treatments, window treatments, paint, design styles, terminology
- knowledge of good sources in your area for furnishings and accessories
- personal integrity and ethical working procedures
- knowledge of practical business procedures, taxes and such
- an entrepreneurial spirit
- an ability to interact gracefully with people, to suggest changes without offending
- knowledge of and a good working relationship with other suppliers of goods and services, such as: painters, paint suppliers, wallpaper hangers, wallpaper suppliers, woodworkers, art companies, framers, and so forth. You don't need to delve into other aspects of interior design if you don't want to, but if you do, you'll be offering a more complete service and it will add additional revenue to your business from time to time.

Remember, you need to perform with solid professionalism in order to be taken seriously by your clients and get the testimonials and referrals you need to sustain your business.

What a Room Arranger (One Day Decorator) Does

An interior room arranger helps the client define the furnishings and accessories for their home, condo or apartment. The consultant will survey the space, ascertain its function, decide on the scope of the project and physically rearrange the furniture and accessories for each room for which the client desires help.

The consultant will make sure that all new arrangements are designed according to solid and respected interior design concepts widely accepted by designers, making sure that the arrangements accommodate the family's activities for each room, keeping traffic patterns open and accessible and creating a total ambience that coordinates with the natural architectural features of the room.

The consultant is often asked additional questions, not related to the arrangement of furniture and accessories, and should be prepared to give professional suggestions.

Consultants also need administrative skills, especially if hired to rearrange an entire home. This could involve the need to hire helpers or the ability to coordinate with workmen from moving companies. They also need to be able to fulfill other functions in operating their businesses, such as telephoning, ordering products, payment of invoices, invoicing, marketing and janitorial services. When you first start out, you have to be able to do it all yourself.

Good public speaking skills may be needed if asked to speak at association gatherings like real estate broker's meetings, seminars and such.

Effective Communication

A good consultant will have excellent communication skills. You'll have to explore your client's goals by asking the right questions and listening attentively for the answers. If you ask the right questions, they will tell you what you need to know. After you have specified the project and have made some design decisions, you'll have to communicate to your client what you propose doing and it's good to include the reasons why. This is particularly helpful to them if you are proposing some major changes in the way the room is arranged.

You need to gently move them in the direction you want to take them, without using intimidating jargon. You need to know what aspects of the project to emphasize so that the client knows what to appreciate about the direction you are suggesting.

After I leave a client, I always send a thank you note, and in that note I always re-emphasize the design concepts used to make the necessary changes. If I have thought of anything else that would be helpful to the client, I always put additional suggestions in that note. I want my clients to know that I didn't stop working for them just because I left the scene.

Being Service Oriented

Always refer to your clients as "clients" and not "customers". Consider the two definitions below:
Customer: a person who purchases a commodity or service
Client: a person who is under the protection of another

When you start to *serve* clients rather than *sell* clients, the limits to your business success will disappear. Don't take the attitude that you are going to sell them a product or service just so you can make the largest one-time profit possible. Take the time to discover and appreciate exactly what they *need.* Once you know the final outcome they need, you lead them to that outcome - in the process you will become their trusted adviser who protects them. This will give them reasons to remain your client for a lifetime.

Clients who trust you will gladly recommend you to others.

I always tell my clients that I am there to "enhance" what they have already begun. Your clients need to know that you are on their "side", that you are really a "team" for the day. You are there to help them solve a problem and you are not there in any judgmental way. I'm always checking with my client as we move along to make sure they are comfortable with the adjustments I am making. If they are starting to get unhappy or uncomfortable, the sooner you spot it the better off you and your client will be.

You don't want to get the whole project completed and then find out that your client just doesn't like the new arrangement. Focus on how you can "serve" them and what additional ways there might be to make their home-life more enjoyable. Give more than you said you would give. When a client believes that you have their best interest at heart, that you are their ally, you will find it extremely easy to service them in the ways you feel most appropriate.

For instance, one client told me that she wanted her three children to be able to run through the living room with ease. She liked an open, simple and airy look. These were critical pieces of information I used later to reinforce to her that I had taken those statements to heart and incorporated them into my decision making process. In order to achieve that goal, I had to adjust some of the design principles I used and "cheat" a little, but remember, I said you need to achieve the goals for the client, as well as improve the arrangements, otherwise they will not keep the arrangement after you leave and will feel they did not get the value of your service that they had expected.

Knowledge of Interior Design Techniques

Just a word about having a thorough knowledge of the mainstream interior design concepts most professionals use. The client is hiring you for your knowledge. She expects you to help her make decisions that are not only good for today but also for tomorrow. She expects you to know what colors look good together and where color is moving over the next few years.

When someone visits her home later, if they aren't complimentary (or worse, critical), the client is going to blame you. She will forget how much she liked it when you first did it. This scenario will probably never happen if you have used solid design principles in the beginning. Basic design concepts will give your arrangements the underlying structure needed for the arrangement to hold up over time. These concepts will not change much through the years.

A firm grounding in interior design concepts will help you develop your client's own taste and visual response. If you don't know why the sofa needs to go in a certain place, if you don't know what the focal point of the room is, and if you don't know "why" it works or it doesn't work, then you will be at a loss to help your client understand. Failing to help your client understand, you will not give her the ability to explain the concept to anyone else who may (kindly or not so kindly) try to influence her in another direction.

The more skilled you are at helping your clients "see" and "appreciate" good furniture and accessory arrangement, the more challenging and exciting your projects will become. You cannot follow (or even break) the rules successfully if you don't know what the rules are.

It's not necessary to go back to college full time to get sufficient knowledge to function well as an arrangement specialist, but some courses and independent study are absolutely essential. Please see Chapter 18 for many additional resources that will help you learn quickly and easily.

But to back your self up even more, enroll in an interior design class at a local community college. Or visit your public library and check out some good design books for independent study. Always be willing to learn. It's important to stay abreast of what's happening in design. Make sure you are subscribing to a couple of good decorating magazines. If you have some design centers locally that are just for the "trade", visit them. If not, walk around furniture stores, wallpaper and fabric stores in your area and check out what's currently popular and available. You just don't know when that information will provide you with the perfect answer to a client's question.

Personal Attitudes

Keep a positive attitude. Confidence in your knowledge and skill and a belief that your services have an inherent value will give you a winning edge. Believe in yourself. As you learn and get experience, your confidence will increase. You'll be able to achieve more in less time.

Your confidence and enthusiasm will be transmitted to your client. A client who is shy about doing something really different from what they are accustomed to will gain boldness and daring and be willing to make the "leap" if you are confident and reassuring. But know when to back off if they are overly reluctant. Probe further to find out what is making them hesitate. You can often overcome objections by simply taking more time to explain.

For all you know, the client may be thrilled with a suggestion personally, but apprehensive about a spouse's anticipated response. It would be good to know this.

Your pride and confidence can be the difference between a professional who lands a few projects and one who lands many or is invited back to service them again. These sentiments, pride and enthusiasm, cannot be manufactured. They are a result of practicing creative problem-solving with your clients and sincerely believing in your talents and the benefits you have to offer.

Your Professional Image

As a professional interior arranger, you are not only selling your expertise, you are selling your good taste and your own personal image. Before you can say a word, as soon as you enter the home, your client begins to evaluate you and whether your personal image is consistent with the image she wants to convey in her home.

It is important for you to project a powerful and successful image of your own, preferably on the same level as your client. Your client will look to you to set a standard of taste in her home, and will want to feel that your style is similar to that of her family.

Your voice, the quality of your wardrobe, your accessories, your marketing materials and your vehicle, all convey a personal message about you. So will the tools you bring with you and the manner in which you transport them.

Make sure your hair is well kept and in a current style. Make sure your makeup is applied appropriately. Keep your fingernails clean. No chipped polish, please. Use deodorant at all times and freshly brushed teeth. Make sure your clothes are appropriate for the project. (I always explain in advance to my client that I will be arriving in my "moving clothes", so that they know to expect me to arrive in more casual attire. This gives them the freedom to "dress down" as well.)

My moving and design tools are all professionally stored in a black "sales" case on wheels. I'll discuss the tools later in another section. But I just mention the case here, because you want to arrive compactly and professionally. A case gives you a neatly organized place to keep your tools while at their home. You want to be able to find things quickly and easily and you don't want to leave anything behind.

Your image is also fashioned by your attitude which was discussed earlier. Bring plenty of confidence and eagerness, a sense of humor, a humble spirit, and eagerness to serve, all mixed with a happy spirit and you will find you are conveying the image of a successful, competent and caring person.

Your Professional Ethics

You will never go wrong in this business (or any business) if you always give your clients MORE than you promise, charge a fair price, offer a guarantee and stand by it 100%, treat clients and vendors the way you would want to be treated, and focus on how you can best serve others.

Homeowners view their consultants as their personal advisors. Therefore, you need to be aware of professional standards of ethics used by other interior design professionals. These standards will probably be the same or similar to all business fields. If you handle your affairs in an honest, ethical manner, you should find your business will develop an excellent reputation within your community and this will enhance your business growth and personal satisfaction.

Sometimes I get asked, "What about selling other products to your clients?" I know of plenty of decorators who offer a Buying Service as well. I personally have always thought of that as a conflict of interest and was not comfortable with the concept. I found it works best for me if my clients have no reason to be concerned about whether or not I will try to sell them anything other than my consultation services and expertise. But it's your business and you can add other services if you wish.

For a few ideas: add a decorating service for homeowners hosting or attending a social event; become a home stager; create beautiful floral arrangements; add window treatments; become a re-designer specifically for persons with a physical disability or select some other niche area to specialize in as well. I started out in design as a graphic designer, and then became a corporate art consultant before I began doing redesign for homeowners. I offer training in almost all of these areas. See the website.

A Word of Advice and a Serious Warning

Some stagers and re-designers ask their clients to leave the home before doing a project. They like the idea of bringing them back later for some kind of "unveiling ceremony". I think this is quite foolish for a couple of reasons and here is how I got there.

1) Any time you're in someone's home all by yourself, you open yourself up to possible litigation and accusations of theft or breakage or other things you're not guilty of doing. In a society where people are quick to sue, this is an unnecessary risk you should weigh carefully before taking a chance. Think about it. You could be accused of stealing something. You could be accused of breaking something. And even if you have insurance, do you really want to have to file a claim or have your client file a claim against your insurance company? If your client is present in the home the entire time you are there, they will be much less apt to think suspiciously toward you because they are there and are aware at all times of where you are and what you're doing. And for you own sake, should you need to enter a private area of the home, you have the ability to request permission to do so before entering. It is much more risky to be left in the home without the owner present.

2) When your client is not there, participating in the process or at least available for questions and answers, you are eliminating a great time of bonding that could be taking place if the client was in the home during the staging or redesign. So I would ask you, "Why would you not want to take advantage of every opportunity to bond with your client that you could get?" Some of my clients have become very good friends. Bonding and making and nurturing a friendship are one of the most important aspects to getting a great testimonial and follow-up referrals that you can have. It seems rather foolish to me to ask the client to leave for any reason especially when it can also be a great learning experience for them. While some clients would rather just leave you to do your thing, many of them will want to be part of the process and see and experience the transformation, and learn as much as they can from you.

3) If your client is not present during the redesign process, you don't have the opportunity to evaluate their feelings or "take their temperature". This can cause negative feelings to arise when you least want them if your client returns to the home and experiences "culture shock". Some people are not as open to drastic changes as others. For these reasons and others, I much prefer to have my client present when I conduct a redesign and that's what I advise you to do as well.

4) On a slightly different note, never call up your competitors and pretend to be a potential client, even if you plan to reveal your real motives later. It is even unwise to do this even if you actually plan on hiring one of them to redesign a room in your home. No one likes the feeling of a "spy" infiltrating their space and asking questions with a hidden agenda. If you want to watch your competition at work, do them the courtesy of announcing your intentions or wishes right up front before you ever ask them a question. Believe me, even if you are successful in any kind of deception, no matter how long you do it, word will get around and impact your reputation negatively. It's not worth it. There is enough work out there for everyone. So don't stoop to spying or pretense to learn this business. It isn't ethical.

Entrepreneurial Skills

Not everyone is cut out to be an entrepreneur. You have to be highly motivated, persistent, professional and persevering. You have to be able to overcome your fears and reservations, learn what you need to learn.

You also need to have the ability to research, assess facts, make decisions, minimize your risks, and be involved in all aspects of your business, getting your hands involved in the "touching and doing" labor.

Entrepreneurs are self starters. They are stubborn, creative and focused. They derive great pleasure from their achievements. They are people willing to be the CEO as well as the janitor. They are flexible, creative, problem solvers.

You can cultivate and develop these skills, but it's best if you've got them naturally. If you have trouble getting up in the morning, if you're a chronic procrastinator, I'm not saying you won't be successful, but you've clearly got to overcome these tendencies. As an entrepreneur, you're not going to make it if you're not willing to sacrifice certain negative traits and "pay the price". I cannot guarantee anyone will make any money in this business. I bring you great training. The action, however, belongs to you.

Initially you'll have to do all of the marketing as well as the running of your business. The most successful business owners, however, in time will be those who eventually spend the majority of their time "marketing" their businesses instead of "running" their businesses.

If you have performed every aspect of your business yourself, however, you'll be able to properly supervise others as your business grows and you begin to delegate responsibilities to employees to handle. So whether you have plans to build a large business or keep it a small home-based consulting service, look at your basic entrepreneurial skills. Take training to acquire ones you don't have.

Finding Your Niche

Clients Who Suit You

Typically potential clients fall into three basic groups: 1) High end clients (upper income level households); 2) Medium end clients (middle to upper income level households); and 3) Low end clients (low income to middle income households).

Generally speaking, your target market for rearrangement design services will be Group 2: medium end clients. High end clients have the ability to hire traditional interior design firms whose practice is to strip everything and start from scratch. This is generally pretty expensive. They aren't going to be looking for simple rearrangement help, in most cases. Low end clients just don't exist. They can't afford your services, won't be looking for anyone who offers what you do, and need to spend their available income on necessities.

So your best target market is homeowners who are middle of the road: they can't quite afford to start from scratch, they need to recycle what they already own, they have a discriminating taste and desire to emulate what they see in decorating magazines, they can afford to spend a modest amount on professional services, such as yours, to achieve a more enjoyable and livable home.

That said, you will need to pre-qualify all prospects. Not everyone who can afford your services is a good candidate for becoming your client. What?

That's right! You don't want just anyone so you want to pre-qualify your prospects. Of course, one of the first areas of pre-qualification will be to make sure they understand your service and the costs to provide your services.

But you also need to make sure that your potential client has enough furnishings and accessories to justify hiring you. Think about it. If someone calls you up and wants you to come to their home to rearrange their furniture, and you get there and they don't own very much and there's very little you can do to help them consequently, and you want to be paid for your time, do you think your client will be very appreciative and speak well of you and your company if you haven't really done anything for them? Of course not.

So you really need to choose your client. They will be making a choice about you too. But it's not a one-way street. Make sure on the front end that your client has sufficiently supplied the room you will rearrange with enough furniture and accessories to give you plenty of things to work with. Otherwise you will both be disappointed in the outcome.

Recently a retired chiropractor called me up in response to my ad in the yellow pages. He had recently moved into a home that he had remodeled. He wanted someone to come to his home and organize his pots and pans and his clothes in his closet. He was prepared to spend no more than $100 for the service.

Well, I don't do "pots and pans", so to speak. And my minimum service call is much higher than $100. He was not a good candidate as a client. So don't let the desire to gain a new client obscure your focus and the minimum goals and policies that you have, hopefully, preset. Define for yourself what type of client you are looking for and what the necessary ingredients and criteria are before you set an appointment.

You can pre-qualify your potential clients over the telephone. I will deal with this subject more thoroughly later in this Primer.

To boil it all down, your niche market is a homeowner who has become frustrated or disenchanted with the way their home (or a room) looks and cannot think of how to arrange it so that it "works". They have tried everything (or nothing) and need a pair of fresh "eyes" to survey the situation and resolve the problem.

Or possibly the homeowner wants you to stage their home in order to sell it, thus wants to present it in the best way possible to stimulate lots of offers. Perhaps the home has been on the market for a while and the owner is frustrated with the lack of offers. Perhaps it is the real estate agent who is pushing for a professional to give the home a nicer ambience.

Or if not needing staging services, possibly the homeowner needs help at the new site with ideas on how to make the old furniture and accessories "work" in the new environment. These are the three major types of scenarios you are most likely to encounter as you begin to develop your business.

Look in your local yellow pages and see if you find any display ads or listing ads for design firms that offer rearrangement services or who specialize just in this type of service. These are your competitors. It wouldn't hurt to call them up as a homeowner just interested in information. Write down the questions they ask you and listen carefully to the way they pre-qualify you. This will not only give you good research for your own use, but it will give you a very good feeling for what *your* potential clients will be curious about in reverse.

If you want to understand someone else, try to walk in their shoes for a while. It will make you much more sensitive to how others feel. Note the things about your competitors that you liked and, equally important, what you didn't like. Keep what was good and make sure you don't make the mistakes that you felt they made.

Finally, do a careful analysis of your business strategy to make sure it matches both your personal goals and the probable needs of your potential clients. Since I came from a background of two entirely different entrepreneurial businesses, both related yet different, it was easy for me to add this service to my already developed services. But we all come from different backgrounds, so make sure you think through and define your "ideal client". Then look for ways to ferret them out of the mass of consumers and don't waste your time looking for and trying to service clients that are definitely outside of that definition.

Distance You Are Willing to Travel

Another consideration you need to make is the distance you are willing to travel to serve a client. When I was actively servicing corporate art consultants, the projects were generally much larger and the potential profit could be huge, considering the time and effort required to complete the project. So it was well worth my time to travel an hour or more away to do a project. But when it comes to my rearrangement services, I'm far more reluctant to travel great distances.

Rearrangement design is typically isolated to just one room in someone's home. It is not that often that a client is willing to pay to have you rearrange an entire home, unless you offer a more complete design service. You're typically going to be spending half a day for one room, counting your travel time. So you need to make some advance decisions with regard to how far from your home or office you are willing to travel and what your time is worth.

It's not just a matter of the worth of your time either. A smart consultant will also factor into the equation the wear and tear on your automobile. Then there's your auto insurance. The price of the gasoline you will use. It's totally up to you how far you are willing to travel. Just make sure that you have predetermined that distance and factor those "hidden" costs into your fee for clients that live some distance away (more on this later).

Chapter Three

About Homeowners

Define a Need

The purpose for decorating one's home is to provide a comfortable, functional and attractive environment for the people who live there. To leave out any one of the three aspects I just listed is to fail the people who live there.

Comfortable - In a day when most people work and are gone from their homes for the better part of the day, coming home should be a pleasant experience. They are tired. They may be irritable. They need to relax. So the more comfortable that experience is, the happier they will be.

Functional - It doesn't matter if the home furnishings are comfortable or not, or whether the space looks beautiful or not, if it does not serve the activities of the family the way it needs to, it has not been decorated properly. Too long consumers have adopted pre-conceived ideas that they must have a "formal" sitting room for guests, a formal dining room for guests or special occasions, and so forth. Not so! I rarely entertain, and I have multiple businesses I run consecutively, so I don't need a formal dining room. Why should I spend precious mortgage dollars providing a space for people who will never be there to use it?

I don't. My "formal" dining room is one of my offices. My breakfast "nook" is where we all eat as a family and on the rare occasion when I do entertain, we serve buffet style or eat outside on an exterior table in the gazebo. This works for me!

So this is another reason to intelligently interview your clients before you begin rearranging anything. You just may find yourself doing them an immense favor by suggesting alternative uses for some of the rooms that will really accommodate their lifestyle rather than "traditional" usages.

Attractive - People want their home to look and feel spectacular, even if the home is small and the furnishings old and well-worn. To walk into a room that is appealing to the eye is enjoyable and inviting. The more attractive it is, the more incentive the homeowner will have to keep it orderly and clean. The more attractive it is, the more other people will enjoy being there.

So whether they realize it or not, most people want their space to include all three of these basic factors. But they don't know how to successfully achieve all three at the same time. Therefore, your first job is to build rapport. The client must feel comfortable in what is essentially a vulnerable situation. The second step is to build your client's confidence in your expertise and your interest in helping to solve any and all problems. Rapport and confidence are the foundations of the consulting relationship. Your job as a consultant, then, will be to give your clients an attractive, comfortable and functional home, using the furnishings they already own. Believe me, it can be done, no matter where they live, and no matter what they have, as long as they have enough items to work with!

It may be necessary to go beyond the surface to find real needs so that you can provide real solutions. The more you know about your client, the family, their future plans, their favorite activities, their hobbies, their habits, the more effective you will be as their rearrangement consultant.

Why Homeowners Need Help

After many years of rearranging other people's homes and visiting homes of family and friends, I have come to the conclusion that most people don't know that their furniture and accessory arrangements are poor, at best.

If you don't know basic design concepts, you might not know that what you've done is ineffective. The most common problems I see are a failure to address a room's natural focal point, failure to create seating arrangements that encourage conversation, failure to balance a room, failure to create a sense of unity, form and rhythm, huge disparities in sizes, failure to account for proportion and scale, failure to acquire a sufficient amount of accessories, failure to properly assess lighting and traffic issues.

So what I find over and over again are homes that look and feel chaotic, disjointed and totally unappealing. I personally wouldn't want to send 5 minutes there, much less live there.

So while most people do a pretty good job of selecting reasonably nice furniture and accessories (to whatever point they have acquired these things), their sense of where to place them leaves much to be desired. So this is why the service of professional room rearrangement is so dramatically and desperately needed. The largest obstacle then is to somehow show homeowners that they need help and that it will be well worth the nominal fee they will pay to receive such a service.

A dear friend of mine, whose home needs a lot of help, was offered a free arrangement service. I didn't want to hurt her feelings, and it's really delicate to try to let someone know that they need help. I knew without a doubt that I could make a dramatic improvement instantly. However, she exclaimed that she had taken some interior design classes in the past and that she knew what she was doing. Sorry to say my free offer of help was not accepted. She doesn't even know that she either didn't understand the concepts she was taught in her classes or that she has forgotten what she was taught.

So this is one of the areas that are a consultant's biggest challenge - convincing people that they have a need that you can dramatically resolve. So either people just don't know they have done it all wrong, or they don't care, or they are secretly frustrated but just don't want to spend the money to have it done right, or their ego blocks their ability to admit they could use some help.

Working with the Decision Maker

You may have noticed that when I write about a client as an individual, that I use the pronouns "she" or "her". This is because I rarely do rearrangement services for men.

When a couple owns a home, more than likely you will be working either with the woman or the couple together, but occasionally you may have opportunity to work with a husband who makes the décor decisions for the family or with a bachelor.

It's important to work with the person who mostly makes the decor decisions for the home. They have the most input to give you and usually are the most vocal and concerned about the final outcome. I've never worked exclusively for anyone but the main decision maker for the home. I would strongly encourage you to keep the same policy.

Occasionally you will have a couple that has differing goals and opinions. This is not an impossible situation, but you need to proceed cautiously and try to find a solution that makes both people happy. Recently the wife, who hired me, found that the changes I made in her room arrangement were quite different from what she had anticipated. She said she was going to have to "get used to it". When I offered to move everything back where it was originally if she was not happy, she said, "Oh no! My husband really likes what you did!"

This is a perfect description of a situation where the client had to let a new and very different arrangement "grow" on her. That's ok, but it's not ideal. I would much prefer for a client to instantly "love" the new look. And that should be your goal, as well. I'll write more about a proper guarantee for you to offer later.

Whenever possible, try to find out if your contact or potential client has the power to pay for your services themselves. If they will need the spouse's permission or joint approval, do not rely on the client to convince the spouse of the need for your services, if possible. They will not be able to properly convey the value of hiring a professional. The spouse may very well think the home is just fine the way it is (men are like that, you know). So whenever possible, try to speak to the spouse yourself so that you can properly represent the perceived value of your services. You will stand a better chance of getting hired.

What Homeowners Need Most

The competition in this specialized service is growing every day. You are wise to be starting your business now while you have a chance to dominate the market in your area. People prefer to deal with people that offer more than one service, however, so you might give thought to other services or products that you could also offer.

While I prefer for my clients to shop on their own for additional furniture or accessories they might need, I do make it clear to them that I can be helpful to them in that area as well should they need me. The fact that I am a published artist lends a great deal of credibility to me when I am discussing the proper arrangement of art. The fact that I have written books on the subject also gives credibility to my expertise and experience. What can you offer that is related to this service? Make a list and add those products and services to your marketing materials.

If there are specific areas of design that you just prefer to avoid, do so. But consider building business relationships with other professionals who would be happy to give you a referral fee to service your clients in those areas. What will separate you from your competitors is your professionalism and service. Traditional design concepts have been around for decades. But the uniqueness of you, your ideas and creativity, your genuine warmth and commitment to service will be observable. Always be professional. Good things will come to you.

Chapter Four

Generating Leads

The best way to generate leads is to put your self in a lead generating mode at all times. A successful consultant, or any entrepreneur for that matter, is someone who will look for leads almost anytime and anywhere. It's a matter of focus and awareness. Make the most of every opportunity. Look for opportunities. Act on them. You'll be amazed at the sources for leads you will garner that go beyond the ones I will discuss here if you are focused and your antenna is up.

If you are constantly looking for new business and referrals, you will help keep yourself from falling into an up and down sales cycle. It's important to be generating leads continuously, not just between projects.

TICKLER FILES - The method you choose must be something that is comfortable for you. It really doesn't matter what method you use, so long as you have some way to store leads and follow up on them in a consistent manner. Some of you will prefer to keep all your data stored on your computer. If you do, be sure to back up your data often. Excel spreadsheets can be effectively used as well as the home office software that comes on your computer.

However, you might prefer to work off your computer. Some consultants enter a lead onto a sheet of paper and then gather as much information as possible. Choose the most promising ones each month and note on your sheets the most likely date to pursue them.

I prefer a 4x6 file box that has two sets of dividers minimum. The first set of dividers is numbered 1-31 for the days of the month. I place my leads on file cards that are 4x6. One lead per card. The leads that I want to follow up on that month are placed behind the day of the month that I plan to make contact.

The second set of dividers is labeled for the months of the year. Those leads that are not ready for follow up until later in the year are placed behind the month that I plan on making contact. At the beginning of each month, I take all the cards behind that month's card and redistribute to the daily dividers.

Remember to record on the card the date, the person you spoke with and the pertinent information discussed immediately following each contact you make. If you want, you could even add more dividers to the back of the box that are labeled according to year. In early January of each year, take the cards behind the upcoming year and redistributed to the monthly dividers, placing the leads for January in the daily dividers.

This is the easiest method I have ever found of storing the original lead information, and keeping my focus on making contact in some way at the appropriate time. I guarantee that if you do not have a lead tracking system in place you will miss out on a lot of business you could have had.

People don't always say "yes" to you right away. Most people need time to get to know you a little and this requires an effort on your part to establish some kind of repetitive contact (be careful not to annoy them). When you have a good lead follow up system, you don't have to shuffle through your leads constantly trying to figure out what to do next. It's organized and it works.

You can buy all of the supplies for a good tickler file at your local office supply store. The file boxes come in plastic or metal. The dividers come pre-packaged and pre-numbered and with the months of the year already printed on them. You can also buy blank dividers. I suggest 4x6 card stock for each individual lead. You can buy these plain or lined, white or colored.

Satisfied Clients

You've probably heard it said, "The best client is one that has been referred to you." Well, I don't know how true that is, but referrals can and will be very important to your business. Your clients can become one of your most valuable sources for leads. Most salespeople will tell you that developing referrals is their best marketing technique. There is nothing quite like the third party endorsement of a satisfied client. It is valuable advertising for you and costs you nothing. If you do your job well, most clients will be happy to enthusiastically recommend your services to others.

History has shown us that fulfilling the client's expectation of a quality product and good service is the number one reason why many of America's top companies are where they are today. The number one formula for success is, "Put the customer first."

Some of your projects will be quick and almost effortless. Others will require much more careful consideration and planning. It can be difficult to predict which projects will need more of your time. So when you encounter a room that is more complex than you anticipated and takes longer to pull together, rather than feeling a bit resentful and trying to think of ways to cut corners or leave before the client is fully satisfied, view it as an investment in your overall marketing efforts. The extra work and time will build goodwill toward future projects.

Consider it an on-going learning process as well. From this experience you will hopefully learn how to ask more probing questions on the front end so that you will be better able to quote the project more realistically. Try to anticipate as much as possible the things that can delay your work or things that could possibly go wrong. Fortunately in this business there isn't much that can go wrong. Other than a delay in meeting your client, an inability to move some piece of furniture when you need to, rearrangement projects generally are pretty smooth.

But there are times when you get surprises. Like the time I offered to rearrange the living room for my pastor's parents. The room turned out to be two rooms in one with nearly 100 family photographs. What was supposed to be a half day project turned into a 1.5 day project. And on top of that, I forgot to take any "before" pictures, so I had a major surprise and a disappointment created by my own forgetfulness.

Those things will happen to you. But just take it in stride because it happens to everyone now and again. This business is one of the most problem free businesses that I have ever been a part of, so keep that in mind.

But back to the subject of referrals. Third party endorsements are not only very effective, but can create an endless chain. But you aren't likely to get referrals unless you keep your name before your satisfied clients in some way.

Here is a brief check list of strategies you can use to create an endless chain of referrals:

- Follow up with visits to the client
- Propose new services that might interest them
- Send thank you notes and presents
- Over time, develop a personal relationship if you can
- Leave brochures and business cards with them before you leave
- Ask for and acknowledge referrals - you have to ask, your clients just don't automatically think to give them to you
- Host or attend parties – these are great places to network, hand out business cards and so forth
- Send periodic notes or newsletters with valuable information to your prospects and clients
- Put your identification on everything you give or send out

Don't be afraid to ask for referrals. People who have been sold on your services will usually be enthusiastic about recommending you to others. If they are reluctant, chances are you don't have a truly satisfied client and you might want to find out why. If there is something wrong, hopefully you can correct it and turn them into a satisfied client. If not, at least you'll know what to avoid in the future. However, there are some people who just don't want to be responsible for recommending anyone ever. There's nothing you can do to change their mind, so don't try. There are plenty of people who will be glad to refer your services. Concentrate on those clients.

Centers of Influence

Centers of influence are people who are probably not your clients but could be. They are typically people who know people - lots of people. They are in a position to contact lots of people on your behalf, or write a letter of recommendation on your behalf that you can send out yourself. Hopefully they are knowledgeable about your services, perhaps in a related profession, such as an architect, a CEO of a furniture store, a CEO of a moving company, owners of real estate companies, highly successful real estate agents. A referral from a center of influence is an excellent way to develop new leads. Make a list of all of the people you know who just seem to know everyone. This is a good place to start. Contact them and ask for a 5 minute meeting to explain what you are going to be offering. Ask them for their help and ideas. People like to be thought of as mentors. If they can help, they usually will want to do so.

If your center of influence is a close contact, perhaps a lunch date would be most appropriate. If you don't feel a brief meeting is appropriate, send them a letter and let them know about your service. Don't look to these people to become clients. See them rather as referrers that may be critical to the success of your business.

Scouts

Many people can serve as "advance men" without any effort on their part. These are professionals in noncompetitive fields who service homeowners. Think about all of the service people who provide goods and services to homeowners. Here is a brief list: landscapers, maid services, mailmen, tree trimmers, babysitters, plumbers, electricians and so forth. These are people that may receive advance notice that someone is going to redecorate or move. Their recommendations to the homeowner, who already trusts them, can be very valuable to you.

Social Events and Leads Clubs

Leads Clubs are groups of salespeople from all fields and industry groups that meet regularly to share leads. Usually they get together for breakfast once a week. As they get to know you and the services you offer, they will consciously remember you as they go about their daily routines. People who attend leads club breakfasts or other types of gatherings know that if they want to receive referrals themselves, they need to be giving out referrals. You will need to be looking always for referrals that you can pass along to others in the group as well. Depending on the type of business you are in, leads clubs can be very profitable or can be a waste of time and energy. Before joining one and paying your membership fee, visit a few times and see if the types of people who are attending are people who are in businesses that deal with homeowners. If the majority of the people work in the corporate or business world, it might not be the best club for you to join. My eBook titled Great Parties is a good trainer on honing your skills at social events.

Yellow Pages

Check out the "Interior Design" and the "Interior Decorator" section of your local yellow pages. See who is advertising and if any of the ads offer a furniture rearrangement service. Chances are no one will be offering that as a specific service. But before you jump in and buy a display ad of any type, look to see how many companies are running display ads. If there aren't very many ads, it means that the yellow pages are not pulling that well. If there are a lot of display ads, you have stiff competition in the category, but the category must be pretty responsive, otherwise your competitors would not be paying out huge amounts of money to advertise there. So this can be a "catch 22". My advise is to work at building your business first through as many "free" methods as you can before you contract for an ad that you have to pay for all year long whether it is good for your business or not.

I do not recommend advertising in any yellow page directory that is not the main directory for the area you want to reach. You also do not want to advertise in any Business to Business directory. Keep all ads directly solely at your target market - homeowners!

Web Sites and Social Media

If you want to be considered professional in the New Millennium you must have a web site. More and more, people are expecting to find your company on the internet. It doesn't matter if it is a small web site or not. The point is you really need to have one. As competition increases, it becomes more important than ever.

I wanted to have complete and instant control over my web sites, so I took a 6 month class at my local community college in web site design. It was one of the best decisions I ever made. There are a lot of software programs that have been developed which will help you create your own web site and do much of the work for you, however, a good knowledge of HTML (the code language for creating most web pages) is very, very useful. I have one of the latest software programs called FrontPage 2000, but I've noticed on many occasions that it injects weird codes from time to time and then my pages don't display properly. Without a strong knowledge of HTML, I would never have been able to figure out what was wrong and correct the problem. I wholeheartedly recommend everyone take a class in HTML. You don't need all of the other training, like JAVA, but you do need to know HTML.

The reason I strongly advocate knowledge of HTML is that I have seen a lot of very poorly designed and constructed web sites put up by "decorators" and "interior designers". You only have a few seconds to impress a visitor to your site. If the site pages are poorly designed, do you honestly think a visitor is going to feel impressed with your skills in the real world? If you're in the business of interior design, you need to have a web site that is nicely designed. I'm not talking about some of those million dollar web sites. Your site might only have 8-10 pages. That's fine. Just make the pages attractive visually. This in itself will go a long way in establishing silently that you know what you're doing when it comes to decorating.

A web site is also great because you can show full color pictures of homes that you have done. Get permission from your clients to show before and after pictures. This will give your business enormous credibility. HTML knowledge will again be a great asset because you can post the pictures yourself and change them instantly whenever you want.

The best quality pictures you will get for your web site are the ones you will take with a digital camera. If you don't have one and can't afford one, see if you can borrow one when you go on appointments. The benefit of a digital picture is that they are virtually "free" to take and you can easily adjust the color and lighting to enhance them if you need to do so. You can display them immediately and don't have any processing and developing fees to pay. Nor do you have to buy film. The one draw back is that they create bigger files due to the better quality. Bigger files take longer to download on people's computers and many people won't wait long enough to see them.

The other way to acquire before and after pictures of the homes you rearrange is with a regular camera. Make sure you have one that will take good quality pictures, particularly in low light situations. Concentrate the majority of your pictures on different angles of the home "before" you rearrange it. Why? Because once you have started work on a room, you will never be able to go back and get more "before" pictures. You could, in a pinch, always go back to a client's home to get "after" pictures, but you can never recapture the home as it was when you first started.

More than once I have been disappointed with the quality of my "before" pictures and had no way to redo them. A few times I forgot to take pictures altogether. Since you don't know at the time you take them what the full extent of their use will be to you later, try to get as many "before" pictures as you can.

The benefit of having photo prints of the homes you have done is that you can then scan these pictures. Scanned pictures usually create smaller files which may not have the quality of digital photos, but will download much faster onto people's computers. What good are pictures of your former projects if no one sees them.

Whether you take your pictures with a digital camera or a traditional camera, you will want to also create a scrapbook of your projects. Periodically a potential client or a referrer will want to see examples of work you have done in the past. Having a professional portfolio of your work will be very impressive. It's a nice keepsake for you as well. After you get really going in your business, you're going to start to forget projects from a long time ago. Your scrapbook will serve as an excellent reminder whenever you need it to. If you just don't have the time or want to take the time to learn HTML and web site design and you have the money, then consider hiring a professional to create a web site for you. But before you take that step, check out their work thoroughly, compare prices (as there is a huge difference in pricing out in the marketplace) and get everything in writing. It's also a very good idea to put all of your ideas down on paper first so that you can give your web developer a real clear picture of just what you want.

If you want to be taken seriously, you should also register your own domain name and have your web site hosted by an Internet Service Provider. Select the ".com" address. Do not fall for putting your site into an "internet mall". Have your own ".com" address and use the email address that comes with your domain as your business email address. In this way, potential clients will not be able to differentiate a small home-based business from a large, commercial brick and mortar business. This gives you, the start up decorator, a level playing field.

It costs a lot less money to launch and sustain a web site than it does to have a yellow page ad. Use your yellow page listing as a place to list your web site. Interested potential clients can then visit your site and really get a good feel for what you offer. It's a lot cheaper and more effective than printing off an expensive brochure which you would also have the expense of mailing out.

I could go on and on about web site development and design, but this is not really the book for that. It requires a book all of its own. By the way, the textbook I used in my HTML class is called: "Creating Web Pages with HTML" by Patrick Carey. You should be able to purchase it over the Internet, but if not you might contact the bookstores at your local colleges to see if they can get it for you. I'm sure there are many other books equally good, but this one has really been helpful to me.

Here's one last thing about web site development. Try to concentrate your whole presentation on the "benefits" your potential clients will derive. Don't confuse "features" with "benefits". Human nature is the same everywhere. People are mainly interested in "what's in it for them". So the more you can translate your service into statements of how it will "help" them, the more successfully you will turn prospects into clients.

If you do not have a FaceBook page or a Twitter account, you might want to get them established as more and more advertising and sharing is done through social media than ever before and I expect this trend to continue.

Personal Observations

Take every opportunity and make the most of it. If you are always in an "opportunity mode", you'll be quite amazed at the number of opportunities that will actually arise. Be willing to talk about your business everywhere to everyone. Talk about what you do at the gym, on the airplane, at a product show, at a social event or civic event. Always have some business cards handy to give out.

Set a goal of collecting a minimum of 5 business cards from other people when you are in a social event. The moment you accept someone else's card, you're free to hand them yours. The moment you have exchanged business cards, there is an implied permission to call them. These people automatically become part of your network and can be good sources of referrals, if you follow up.

Any activity that puts you in contact with homeowners will be good for your business. Get involved in community activities of interest to you or members of your family. Look at your personal style and formulate a business marketing strategy that suits your style.

Personally, I'm very comfortable speaking in public or teaching a class or seminar. But I am not comfortable with chatting at social functions and would never include a cocktail party as part of my marketing plan. But you might be just the opposite. Try to stretch yourself outside your comfort zone from time to time, but concentrate your marketing efforts in the manner and ways that suit your personal style.

New Buyer's Lists

Depending on where you live, you might consider subscribing to a list composed of new homeowners. These are lists compiled by businesses that are in the profession of creating all types of lists. You would want to zero in on a specialized list of homeowners in a certain locale, who own homes in a certain price range. They can be new owners or established dwellers, so long as they are in the income bracket that can afford a service such as yours.

Before buying a huge number of names and addresses, you should run small tests to see if the list is "clean" and current and to get a feeling for your marketing strategies on how to approach the owners. Never jump into any marketing strategy without testing it first. Again, when starting out, try to use the "free" strategies first. You may never need to purchase lists and leads and pay for expensive advertising if you work the other methods diligently and effectively.

Moving Companies

Just as real estate agents and brokers are in touch with homeowners who are in transition, so are moving companies. Visit the moving companies closest to you and try to establish some rapport with the owner or salespeople. Explain your services; tell them about your web site; offer to refer business to them as you run across people. Perhaps the moving company will be happy to hand out a brochure or flyer to everyone who rents a moving van or hires their service. You could offer a special price to anyone who contacts you for service as a result of being referred by their moving company. This is an excellent way for the moving company to generate more good will and be well remembered favorably after you do an outstanding job of arranging the homeowner's furniture in their new location.

Home Staging

I've already mentioned the importance of including home staging services as part of your overall plan. I don't want to belabor the point, but if you do you will find that this service can be a very good source for redesign business. Every home that is sold in your area involves a seller and a buyer. Both parties are then going to be moving into a space that is "new" to them, bringing their furniture and accessories with them from a previous dwelling. They will need your help. If you are the stager on the project, you stand a much better chance of picking up this additional revenue than if someone else staged the home or if the home was prepared by the seller or the seller's agent. (For training on developing a home staging business see the last chapter.)

A System of Getting Regular Referrals

When you enter the consulting field, and you are a staging or redesign consultant, you will quickly realize the value of getting referrals from your clients, your prospects, people you know, family, friends, co-workers, other trades people, and so forth. Referrals are very powerful and help to grow your business and sustain your business. But getting referrals doesn't happen automatically. You've got to take a pro-active approach and put systems into place that help you generate them. Here is one of the best systems you can utilize.

It's a system of sending out regular greeting cards to people you want to stay in touch with. I recently decided to award the refinance of my home to a mortgage broker who consistently sent me greeting cards. His approach was very, very low key. Since it wasn't by email or phone, I never got upset when I received his periodic greeting cards. What he was doing was reminding me, ever so gently, and every so often that he was still in business and ready to help me if I needed him. So after getting his cards a few times, and when the timing was right, I contacted him to handle the processing of my loan application. If you will capture the power of sending out greeting cards to the people you want to do business with and people you want to refer business to you, you will go a very long way in building, growing and sustaining your business for the long term.

But I've got a powerful system developed by some very shrewd marketing people who have put together a system that makes sending out greeting cards so easy you can do it faster than doing it yourself. All you have to do is visit **www.sendoutcards.com**. You'll be able to see how the system works and just how easy it is to send out greeting cards for any occasion and purpose to anyone you want to send them to. You'll love this system. You don't have to stock cards, you don't have to have stamps on hand or take the mail to the post office. It's all done for you over the internet. And you can even customize the cards with your signature and picture if you like. I use it in my own business and have found it to be very helpful, a time saver and very powerful marketing tool.

Encourage referrals from other types of companies: home furnishing retailers, painting and wallpapering businesses, home decorating centers, builders, fabric centers, floor covering retailers, window treatment retailers. Place classified ads in local and regional newspapers and magazines. Rent a booth at home furnishings shows.

Develop a Strong Career Book or Portfolio of Your Work

When you get more and more projects under your belt, you'll have enough put together to create a strong and powerful portfolio of your work. Carry a small album with you at all times or keep in your car so you're always ready to show prospective clients how you've been able to help other people. Put your website or other type of identification on your photos with an image editing software program of your choice. Many computers come with some type of editing software these days. Heck, you can even use your cell phone nowadays to alter photos and make them look more professional and attractive. Just don't go overboard. Can you see how effective before and after pictures are and how well they will tell your story for you? Even in black and white, you can see the improvement.

BEFORE — China cabinet needs de-cluttering. The client had just randomly placed items on the shelves without much thought.

AFTER – Grouping like-kinds together, the arrangement is fantastic now and really made a huge improvement. Now it is a source of pride and enjoyment for the client.

Chapter Five

Getting the Appointment

You Make the Contact

I totally hate it, as a homeowner myself, when I get calls from salespeople. If I hate being bothered by sales pitches over the phone, I can imagine other people feel the same way. I do not recommend making cold calls to homeowners. If you do, you need a really thick skin! You will find a lot of rejection and you may even encounter people who will be irritated at you.

Under no circumstances should you resort to a computer to dial your phone numbers for you. You will just generate negative reactions and your business cannot afford to start off making ill will all over the area.

The only people I ever call by telephone are people who have called me to request a return phone call, people who have been referred to me by people they know and trust, or business people with whom I would like to interact for the purposes of gaining or giving referrals.

But it's your business and you can handle it any way you please. I'm just saying that a negative response will travel a lot farther by word of mouth than a positive response. So try to treat homeowners the way you would like to be treated. Then your good reputation will precede you and you never have to be concerned about overcoming a negative reputation.

The Prospect Contacts You

When a prospect contacts you, try to find out as soon as possible how they found out about you. This is important because you're going to want to track your marketing methods in some way to know which strategies are good and which ones needs to be dropped. So I am trained to ask very early in the conversation about where and how they heard about me.

Before you get to the point where people are calling you, however, you should spend some time in advance of thinking through the kinds of things you wish to say to a prospect over the phone. Paramount to your thinking should be your USP. A USP is your "unique selling proposition". It needs to be specific and have a clear benefit that you are offering to your prospects.

You need to think carefully about your fee structure and have a clear picture of what you will charge for your service, how much the charge will be altered by the distance you have to travel, whether you have a minimum charge, flat rate or hourly fee, how long you anticipate a project will take. The reason you need to have all of this information well thought out in advance is that you are surely going to be asked specific questions. You do not want to hesitate with your answers. If you are hesitant, the prospect is going to get hesitant as well and you will surely lose the appointment. Hesitation makes you appear unprofessional and silently suggests you either don't know what you're doing or that you are creating a special price or stipulation just for them. They will undoubtedly suspect that the price is higher.

So predetermine as much as you can what your answers will be to the questions you will undoubtedly be asked.

Here are some of the typical questions that prospects ask:

- Can you tell me what your service is all about?
- How long does it take?
- What do you charge?
- What is your experience or expertise?
- Do you actually move my furniture?
- Do I need to be here?

Most of the time you'll discover their priority questions will relate to what you charge. The beauty of being self employed is that you can charge whatever you want to charge. But it should be affordable and competitive. If you charge too little, the prospect might think you're not really a professional. If you charge too much, they just won't see the value or might not be able to afford that much. So you need to be affordable, yet professional. This can be tricky and you may have to experiment for a while until you find a price that the market in your area will bear.

If the prospect tells you that they want to think about it or that they have to discuss the matter with a husband, spouse or additional person, chances are they either cannot afford your price or you have failed to get them to understand the value and benefit of having you serve them.

I'm not a pushy salesperson. I hate it when people get pushy with me and I refuse to do that to others. I can tell you from experience, however, that if someone doesn't hire you on the spot and set an appointment for you to come to their home, you're not going to get them at all. I've never had one person call me back after telling me they needed to talk to someone else or think about it further. It just doesn't happen.

But that doesn't change how I respond to them. No matter what they tell me, I'm always pleasant, I always try to be as informative and helpful as I can be, and I treat them as I would want to be treated. You must understand that people do not want to say, "Well, I can't afford you." No one likes to say "no". So they say "maybe" instead. A "maybe" is nothing more than a disguised "no".

Don't fret! There are millions of homeowners who are all potential clients. If the person who cannot afford your services takes a pass, they might know other people who would love to hear about your services. If you are kind, friendly, enthusiastic and helpful, no matter what their response is, it will come back to you in the future. Entire businesses have been built off of the referrals from just one or two people.

Direct Mail Letters, Flyers and Brochures

Business that you generate from your direct mail flyers, letters and brochures is bonus business. You can build a successful business without them, but they will enhance your business if you have them. They will help you set out your credentials and help you identify what is unique about you, thus separating you from your competition. You can mail them out or hand them out. They are all seeds that you are planting in your local area. Any one of them can result in a referral that you may or may not know anything about.

I suggest that you set aside a small portion from every project you do to cover the cost of developing your marketing strategies, no matter what form they take. The old saying, "It takes money to make money" isn't true in every situation, but you do need to be prepared to reinvest a portion of your earnings back into your business to help it grow.

For more help in planning and developing direct mail pieces, flyers, letters and brochures, consult your local library. There are a lot of good books on marketing strategies. Take time each week to continue to educate yourself in the area of marketing. It will pay off for you in the future, if not immediately. I have also listed some good references and resources at the end of this Primer.

When sending a letter, don't try to pitch your whole service or product in the letter. Briefly introduce yourself, state some quick benefits and features, and invite them to contact you (unless you have a way to follow up yourself). Save the "sales pitch" for the first appointment or at least the first phone call where the client will be able to pick up on your friendly voice and enthusiasm. It's impossible to convey those feelings in a letter. So don't try to do anything more in a letter than peak their interest.

Here is part of a sample introductory letter:

"Dear _____,

I noticed the other day that you are new to the area and I want to especially welcome you to the neighborhood. I know a lot of people who move into a new home and bring their furnishings from a previous home to use in the new space. Sometimes that's really difficult to do.

I thought you might be interested to know that I specialize in helping people adapt the older furnishings and accessories to the new space by providing a very affordable professional room arrangement service." . . . .
then go on from there.

You get the idea.

Keep the letter simple and straight forward. Remember that it should be laden with benefits and how you can make life better for them quickly and easily.

At the end of the letter say something like,

Don't try to cover too much ground in your letter. Peak their interest, give them multiple ways to get more information and thank them for considering your services for themselves or for passing the information along to someone else they know.

Business Cards

If you don't use your personal name in your business name, then you will need to choose another name to call your business. This is called a DBA, which stands for "Doing Business As". I will discuss how to set up a DBA later in this Primer, but for now I just want you to think about choosing a name for your business that is descriptive of what you are offering.

A lot of businesses choose names that are so non-descriptive or confusing, they are poor marketing choices. The best names are the ones that tell people instantly something about what your company specializes in and that are easy to pronounce on the phone. That way your name is a mini billboard, working for you wherever people see it.

So stay away from vague, non-descript names that don't tell anyone at a glance something about what you are offering.

Phone Discussions

A young woman left a message on my voice mail yesterday requesting more information and a return phone call. I called her back this morning and we had a pleasant conversation. She had a number of questions which I answered enthusiastically and in a positive, benefit driven way. She had seen my ad in the yellow pages and had also seen the concept of one day decor on a cable TV station. The conversation flowed easily because she already had a working understanding of the concept. Unfortunately I believe the service was a little beyond her pocket book. This will happen even though you've done everything you can to explain the benefits and features and assured the prospect that you will do everything in your power to help them in any way possible.

There are some people who are convinced that a service of this kind should be offered barely above "free". Don't devalue what you have to offer someone just to get a project. Believe it or not, I have received some of the worst instances of ingratitude from people whose homes I rearranged completely FREE! You would think they would have been delighted and totally excited about giving you referrals. Unfortunately, it's part of human nature to take for granted and devalue what is received free.

So it's not surprising that even though I spent hours of my time and dramatically improved their home in every way, the people who received the service for free were the least grateful "clients" I have ever had. You can offer to do the homes of close friends or family if you want to so you can get some practice and get some good before and after pictures to use, but once you have a few projects under your belt, charge for the service after that. You deserve to be paid for what you provide.

There are people who will be happy to pay for the service out there. You just have to get the word out in a consistent and persistent manner. Don't give up if it's slow at first.

Typically this is a one-appointment business. I really don't involve myself with going to the home to make a formal presentation to get them to hire me. I know that some arrangers do this, but I find it a waste of time and time is a premium with me due to all of my other business activities.

I've also found that if someone can't get a good idea of what you can do for them over the phone or by looking at your web site, you're probably never going to convince them (or their spouse) anyway. Some other professionals might disagree with me. It's really your choice. If you feel you can be effective in person and want to take the time to return a second time to do the work, go for it.

But if you choose this method, beware of the prospect that pretends to be interested to get you to their home. They may have a secret agenda to pick your brain while you are there, send you away without a project and then use the ideas that you gave them for free. This happens. If you find yourself in a situation where someone is trying to get you to reveal your thoughts and ideas without actually "hiring" you, refrain from the temptation to "strut your stuff". Kindly explain that your ideas and creativity are your "products" and you cannot give them away for free.

Confirmation Call

After you make an appointment, it's a very good idea to call the client the day before to reconfirm the appointment. Yes, it's an opportunity for the client to back out of the appointment altogether, but better for them to back out than for you to travel to their home only to have them gone. That's a complete waste of your time. In this confirmation call you also want to re-convey to the client that you will keep the appointment and that you operate on a professional level.

It's also a good time to ask any questions that you want to ask that you may have neglected to ask when the appointment was set. You can also use this time to restate what you plan to do and remind the client of anything you want them to do prior to your visit.

I have found it advantageous, at least at times, to request that the room I am to rearrange be thoroughly cleaned prior to my visit. You don't want to have to take time to clean the room as you move things. You're not their maid. So mention at the outset that you would appreciate it if the room is thoroughly cleaned in advance. Stress how much time this will save once the rearrangement process starts.

Regarding Cancellations

I've never, never had any one cancel and offer me money anyway. Never! I've had plenty of cancellations though. I think you'll shoot yourself in the foot if you insist up front on a cancellation fee, personally. You might scare away someone that would have booked otherwise. But it all depends on how much of a cancellation problem you have. If it happens all the time, then you might want to protect yourself. If it seldom happens, don't worry about it. If you had to turn away an appointment, that puts another slant on it. My philosophy was that I'd just as soon stay at my home office, so I didn't much care one way or another if I got a cancellation.

I try to operate as much as possible from the point of view: When in doubt, don't. Also, I try to put myself in their shoes. If the cancellation reason is legitimate and can't be helped, that's one thing. Let it slide. If it's fishy, that's another thing. I had a lady cancel about 4 days before a full redesign I was going to do last Tuesday. I wasn't surprised, because I myself had told her that since my specialty was in working with what she already owns, and she plans to buy a lot of new furniture, that it probably wasn't in her best interest to have me come. I gave her about ½ hour of free advice on the phone. When she cancelled, I wasn't surprised and I directed her to my web site instead. She wound up signing up for my newsletter and getting additional design training. I should get some nice referrals from this lady. And I leave the situation feeling like I did something very valuable for another human being.

Regarding a cancellation fee, even if you state it or have it in a written agreement, that doesn't mean they will pay it. Then you're left taking them to court. Will it be worth your time to pursue it? If you offer credit card purchases, you could insist that they purchase the booking immediately on line or by giving you their credit card information to process manually. Then if they cancel you refund a portion of the fee and keep the rest as the cancellation fee.

I personally have never had a cancellation fee if they call me before I leave home. Now if I got to their home and they weren't there, I'd be mad enough to go after them, which is why I always confirm appointments the day before. But you have to have stated a cancellation fee up front to be successful. In my art consulting business, I would charge them if I went and spent time pulling a proposal together and then they backed out after giving me a green light. I had to sue two corporations for that and got my money both times without having to go to court. But we were talking several thousand dollars in one case and several hundred in the other. I don't care about residential cancellations because I always have a Plan B and I never book more than one redesign in a day.

So it's a tough call. If I told them about a cancellation fee, I would wait until I had the date and time all set with them. Then tell them that if they should wish to cancel, there will be a penalty and explain why. If they simply postpone and set up for the following week, I would not penalize them. I try to walk in their shoes. You can't go wrong by not charging them, but adding them to your mailing, etc. they may still become your client at a later date and in the meantime speak highly of you because you didn't penalize them.

Just the other day, I went to pick up our car from a dealership where we had submitted it for repair. When I got the report back from them, it was ridiculously high and we decided to pull the car and take it to our regular mechanic. We only took it there because my husband thought it was a computer problem.

When I went to pick it up, they wanted $120, at which I balked. The man came in and told me they always charge for diagnostics whether you have them do the work or not, that all dealerships do that. Well, I had expected to pay something, but not $120. So I told him that then he should have mentioned that to us at the outset and told us how much the diagnostics would be. He didn't and, therefore, there was no verbal contract with us to pay for diagnostics. There was nothing in their written contract as well. He tried to find something in writing and couldn't. So then he offered to lower it to $80 and that's where we ultimately settled though I argued for $60. I can understand giving them some money for their trouble, but $120 was too much. I got my car and left. However, it left a bad taste in my mouth, and so I am never going to do business with that dealership again, and I'll forever relate this story to other people as well. So, over $80, they may ultimately lose more than either they or I realize.

So the bottom line is this. How much negative talk do you want floating around about you and your business, even if you have a right to be compensated? You have to make that call. People will always, always spread bad news faster and farther than good news. And they will probably embellish the bad news and downplay the good news. But by the same token, you want to minimize your damages as much as possible. So I think you should keep the problem in mind, put nothing in writing, and judge each case individually. If your client is somewhat hesitant to book the appointment, then mention the cancellation fee. If they are very excited and enthusiastic about having you come, don't mention it, because if they cancel, more than likely they will reschedule anyway.

Some times the culprit is not the person, but the spouse or friend who later says, "You booked an appointment for her to do WHAT????? It's going to cost you WHAT??????" It always helps me to remind myself that my business is in God's hands, and that He knew there was going to be a cancellation and He was not surprised by it. And since my business all belongs to Him anyway, what would He want me to do about the cancellation and my unexpected free time?

Furniture Style and Color Palette Pre-Check

I already mentioned the need to ask sufficient questions over the phone to get a better feeling before you set out as to the scope of the project you will most likely be doing. One of the more important questions that I always ask at the time I set the appointment, or on my confirmation call, is regarding the color palette and the style of their furniture.

It really doesn't matter to me what their colors are, nor what their style is. But I like to know in advance so that I can be prepared with information regarding color or style, sources and such that might be helpful to them. The other reason is because I want to get an idea as to how much they already own just in case I need to bring some extra things with me.

Taking Extra Accessories Along

Once I know what colors my client is decorating with, I will look around my studio or home for accessories that I might take with me to help give my client an idea of how accessories will enhance the space if I get the feeling the home is fairly sparse.

Many people have not collected enough accessories to really arrange a room properly. The products they mostly do not have enough of are: framed art, pillows, plants and table top ornaments. Many people have trouble visualizing and it really helps to have some extra accessories in their colors and, hopefully, their style to incorporate into the final arrangement so they can "see" how attractive they would be.

You're not going to sell them these accessories, just show them how much they will add to the finished look and encourage them to add these types of accessories. One of my clients went out the next day and purchased a tree and a console because she saw the dramatic benefit of having them. While my goal is always to complete a room using only the things they already own, this is a goal but not always the reality.

I also like to have plenty of additional accessories in the trunk of my car so that if I need something to fill in or camouflage an unsightly part of the room so that my "after" pictures look more complete, I will have something to add just for the picture.

AFTER – Small grouping over fireplace allows the client to display as much as possible while still keeping the room from becoming cluttered. A strong ability to design attractive wall groupings for your client will help you include much more of their treasures into the room so that it truly reflects their personality, not yours. This is not about making your "stamp" on a design esthetic. It's all about maximizing the furnishings your client already has and giving them a refreshing new way to display what they own in a more attractive manner while making the room much more functional.

Chapter Six

Your Arrival

Consultant Etiquette

There are a few rules of proper etiquette which you should abide by. Always remember that you are going to someone's home, their private space. No matter how long someone has lived in their home, they attach special feelings to their home, their furniture, their accessories and their family members. There are two primary "no fly zones" that you should note, as well as three other important things to do..

BE ON TIME - Just as you value your time, your client values hers. Be considerate and arrive on time. Do not arrive early, unless you have indicated in advance that you might be early. I hate for someone to come to my home before I am ready to receive them, so don't do it to someone else. If you arrive early, sit in your car and wait until the appropriate time to ring the doorbell. The homeowner will be grateful.

PARK ON THE STREET - A person's driveway is their private space. Do not invade this space. Even though they don't say anything, they will prefer for you to park on the street.

When I make an appointment, I always inquire about parking. This is from my years of working as a corporate art consultant where I was dealing with high rise buildings and usually limited parking places where I had to pay for parking. So I always want to ask about where to park.

Even if the homeowner tells me to just park in their driveway, I never do unless there just isn't any where else to park. Why? Because I never know if someone else in the family is going to arrive home and become irritated at someone parked in their space or what they perceive to be their space.

This is especially important if your car has a fluid leak of any kind. You definitely do not want your car to spew out something on their driveway. So make a habit of parking on the street. Parking is usually not a problem at most homes.

COMPLIMENT THE HOMEOWNER IMMEDIATELY - I don't care if you have just walked into the most awful house you have ever been in. If you look for it, there will always, always be something that you can genuinely compliment the homeowner for - even if it is not the home. Compliment them on the easy directions they gave you, the neighborhood, the front garden, the entry, the colors they have decided to decorate with, her hair, her family -- I don't care what it is regarding, find some way to compliment the owner. Be genuine, however. They will know if you are being phony. Try to be as specific with your compliment as possible. It will have more meaning if you are specific. I can live on a good compliment for a month. So can other people. So quickly look for one or more things you can comment on and greet the client with a huge smile. More on this later.

ASK FOR PERMISSION - Where ever you go in the house, ask permission first. This is a person's private dwelling. Do not presume that you can go any where you please. Be particularly sensitive to going into the person's bedroom or private bath. These are just areas to stay away from unless invited to enter.

HANDLE THINGS CAREFULLY AND GRACEFULLY - You are going to be working with the personal possessions of your client. You are going to be involved in moving furniture and accessories. You definitely do not want to damage anything. Some of the furnishings are going to be heavy, some are going to be delicate.

This is another good reason to ask questions in advance. One of the questions you will want to ask before going is whether there is a TV in the room you will be rearranging. If there is a TV, you're going to need to know if it can be safely moved to another part of the room. Often the TV antenna or cable is such that the TV must stay right where it currently is, whether or not it is good for the design of the room.

If there are some really heavy or difficult furnishings, like a large buffet, armoire or entertainment center, you need to set the appointment for a time when the client can have a man present to do the heavy work. I don't know about you, but I can't move things that are extremely heavy nor do I want to try.

In addition to this, I try not to be the one that moves electrical equipment or anything else that could be harmed easily by movement. It is a good practice to let the owner move the things that are most at risk. You don't want the liability of that to fall on you.

I have never broken a client's possession, partly by being extremely patient and careful of what I am doing. But there's always the first time waiting to happen. Breaking something can have a drastic affect on your entire relationship with this client. Be careful. I will discuss a liability waiver form you need to have them sign later in this Primer.

Tools of the Trade

Here is a list of the main tools of the trade that I always take with me on an appointment:

* My portfolio (I usually don't need it, but always good to have it if I do)
* A 25' metal measuring tape
* A set of **"furniture sliders"** - plastic discs (which come 4 sliders per set) that you can place under heavy furniture and slide over carpeting or hard floors to move furniture easily and almost effortlessly (See http://www.decorate-redecorate.com/furniture-movers-carpet.html) for the ones to use on carpet. See http://www.decorate-redecorate.com/furniture-movers-hard-floors.html for sliders for hard surfaces.)
* A paint chip sampler (I use Behr paints, Dunn Edwards Paints & Glidden's fan decks)
* A note pad or 1/4" graph paper, pencil or pen
* My wide angle digital camera (primary camera)
* A wide angle lens traditional camera and tripod
* An artificial tree
* Assorted artificial plants of various sizes in baskets
* An assortment of other accessories in the colors my client is decorating with, if I have them
* A Thomas Brothers map (or written directions from MapQuest.Com)

- A liability waiver form
- An invoice
- A client card
- A testimonial and referral request sheet
- A professional sales case on wheels (available at Staples, Office Depot, Office Max)
- A dust cloth
- Deodorant
- Allergy pills (if you are allergic to dust mites)
- Clean white cotton gloves
- Clean white soft cotton rags
- Padded trays for carrying small objects at one time
- A padded dolly
- A supply of cardboard or foam core sheets to protect works of art

---

Extra furniture sliders - It never hurts to have more than one set. I always take several sets with me on appointments. You'll quickly see that you'll want to move several pieces of furniture in sequence. If you have more than one set, you can do that without having to constantly move the set from one piece to another and back again. See Chapter Eighteen for these.

Carry as much as you can in a professional sales case on wheels or in some other enclosed case. Do not walk in to anyone's home carrying your tools in your open hands or in a box. This will instantly devalue your credibility. Even though you will be dressed casually because you are going to be doing physical labor while there, you want your appearance and everything you bring to be professional and organized.

First Impressions

Someone once said, "I can tell the second I meet someone whether I want to do business with them. The rest of the time with them is spent justifying my first impulse." Whether you realize it or not, we all gather first impressions and once gathered, they are hard to change. That's why you want to create a good first impression.

Your wardrobe and personal image are the first step toward creating rapport with the client when you arrive at the home. Up until that time, you have conversed over the phone; you may have sent them literature; they may have visited your web site. Each time they have seen something generated by you they have added information to their list of impressions.

Normally I would be advising you to wear business-like attire, but this is a different kind of business. It would be inappropriate for you to show up in a dress and heels or a suit, as the case may be. You have sold your services on the premise that you will physically be moving their furniture and accessories. So it makes great sense to arrive in casual attire that makes it possible for you to do the work you are hired to do. But I would definitely state to my client over the phone to expect to see you in your "furniture moving" attire, whatever you choose for that to be.

I recommend slightly loose fitting attire, not overly baggy, but loose enough to be comfortable - clothing that will allow you to bend over easily, reach easily, or push and pull easily.

I recommend comfortable shoes that tie on. You don't want to worry about a shoe coming off while you are moving something or carrying something. You certainly don't want to trip over a lost shoe, but nor do you want to trip over shoelaces. So it's a good idea to double knot your laces. I like to wear shoes with plenty of cushioning. In any half day appointment, you can figure in advance that you're going to be on your feet most of the time, so you definitely want your shoes to be well padded and as comfortable as possible.

After introducing myself and giving out my opening compliments and stating how glad I am to be there, I always look for an out of the way place to store my case of tools. I leave the extra accessories in my car until I know for sure I will need them, and only then do I make trips to the car to bring in additional things.

So within 60 seconds I am ready to begin. I don't like to waste my client's time nor mine, so I come prepared to begin immediately.

Gaining Control

Now this can be a tricky part. Even though this is my client's home, and in essence I am a guest while there, I am also the consultant with the expertise, so it is important to take leadership with regard to what is to happen next.

Often my client is running a little late and has some things to do yet, like tidying up the kitchen, getting kids squared away and so forth. So you will have to play it by ear and decide which option to go for first: either a walk thru of the home, particularly the room the client wants you to address, or whether to tell the client that you first would like to take some "before" pictures, with their permission.

I have never had a client say "no, you can't take pictures" or "no, I'd rather you do this or that". They are always relieved, I think, for you to assume control over what will happen next. So while I am going to discuss taking "after" pictures a little later in this sequence, this could certainly be an appropriate time to actually take the "before" pictures. It's really going to depend on what you sense from the homeowner after you first arrive.

Doing a Walk Thru or Shopping the Home

If it has not already been decided which room you will be working on, it would be a very good idea to ask the client to see the whole house. If she seems a little reluctant at first, reassure her that you don't care if it's messy (that she should see yours) and that you just want to get an idea for her personality and taste.

It is a good idea at the time of your re-confirmation phone call to mention you will want to do a walk thru of the whole house and give the reasons (shopping the home to see what could be used from other areas to complete the room you're working on). This advanced "warning" allows your client to tidy up and possibly avoid some embarrassment on her part. She will appreciate the "heads up".

Even though you may be hired only to rearrange one room, there might just be furniture and accessories in another room that you'll elect to "borrow" and place in the room you are working on. You won't have that option if you don't see the other rooms and get a feel for the full scope of their possessions that you could consider including in your redesign.

So it's a good idea to ask the client to give you a walk through of the entire home. In the process of doing that, have the client point out any furniture or accessories that she will allow you to consider moving to another room. Find out if there are any furnishings and accessories in these other rooms that she definitely wants to remain in the rooms where they are presently located. This way you will have a better understanding of what will be available for your use.

There are many times when a client will own something that will be perfect for the room you are working on but has never considered using it in that room. People tell me all the time, "I never would have thought of putting that there." So make mental notes of all the pieces you can consider decorating with, not just the things that are in the room at the time you begin.

Write down the measurements of any pieces you instantly know you're probably going to want to use or at least consider using. Once you're involved in the actual moving of furniture, you might easily forget if you haven't written it down.

What to Do First

The Initial Interview

As I have stated earlier, the goal of every consultant/arranger should be to create a space for the client that is visually appealing, comfortable and functional. In order to do that successfully, you're going to need to ask your client some specific questions.

Why questions? Questions give you critical information, help verify assumptions and clarify understandings. They involve the prospect, reveal her interests and those of her family; they help you understand her priorities, the family's special agendas and their personality style. They help you re-qualify her as the correct decision-maker, and just as importantly, they let you demonstrate your interest in her and her home.

It's very important that your client believes that you understand her and what is important to her. This is far more important than her understanding who you are and what you do. Do not underestimate the importance of sitting down with your client at this point and asking specific questions.

Choosing the Room

The first question you're going to need answered, if you don't know already, is which room the client wishes you to work on. Most of the time you will be hired to do only one room - and most of the time that room will either be a living room or a family room/den. It is usually the room that people "live" in the most. This is usually the room they care about the most because they use it constantly and they have usually purchased more furniture and accessories for this room. It is also the room that will usually be the messiest, disorganized and frustrating to the homeowner. So if you don't know at this point where you will be working, ask. The novice might look at this room and think it looks ok, but in reality it was extremely spacey and so uncomfortable for the family, they never used the room except at Christmas, and then only because the Christmas tree was placed in the room.

If the client isn't sure and wants some input (which I have never had happen), then you should choose the room where you feel you can make the most dramatic transformation to improve the home, such as I did here. If you have been hired to do the entire home, I recommend that you start with the entry and the high focus rooms (rooms used by the family and guests), then work your way through the home until you have completed the private rooms. Once the room selection has been made you're ready to interview the client.

AFTER REDESIGN - Here is how the room came out once I rearranged the furniture. The two sofas were gorgeous, even though quite old. They were both the exact same length making them ideal to be place opposite each other. A lovely TV cabinet had been rather hidden at the opposite end of the room. Anyone wanting to watch TV had to sit on the floor or bring in a chair. Very awkward indeed. In the client's configuration, the beautiful coffee table served only those seated on one of the two sofas. In my arrangement, the coffee table now serves anyone seated on either sofa. A beautiful sofa table was placed against the wall behind the right sofa, which helped to anchor the beautiful set of four carvings already on the wall. I changed the contemporary lamp out for a more Asian style and rearranged two groupings on the TV cabinet. The white carpet had numerous stains and by repositioning the two sofas in this configuration I was able to cover up many of the stains. Do you agree the room looks much more attractive and function now?

After Redesign

Client's Needs and Clarifications

Here are some specific questions you might consider asking at this point to help you understand your client and the needs of the family. These are not the only questions you might ask but will, hopefully, serve as a starting point. Continue to ask questions and get feedback until you feel you comfortably have enough information to proceed.

STARTER QUESTIONS

- Tell me a little about your family.
- What are the main activities that the room is used for
- Who uses the room the most
- Do you entertain much
- How often do you entertain
- Besides your immediate family, what different kinds of people visit your home
- What special values do you want your home (or room) to express to visitors
- What image do you wish to project
- What future plans do you have for the room or home
- What is the timing on your future plans
- Are you happy with the colors in the room now
- If you are not happy, what would you like to change
- Which furniture pieces in the room are you most happy about
- Which furniture pieces in the room do you least care about
- Are you open to pulling furniture and/or accessories from other parts of the home into this room
- Do you see the activities for this room changing in the near future
- Are you anticipating any significant changes in your family soon (empty nest, additional child, relatives moving in or out, etc.)
- Are you planning any major purchases of furniture soon that would affect this room
- Has your spouse communicated any specific requests or concerns to you that I should know about (assuming the spouse is not present)
- Is there anything in the room particularly breakable or that presently needs repair (have client remove all breakable things AFTER you take your "before pictures")

Depending on the responses of your client, you might not need to cover any more probing ground than what these questions trigger. But you'll probably find that the answers to these questions will trigger other questions not covered here.

Questions can also be useful in confirming your understanding of what your client wants and needs from you. Those questions usually begin with, "Let me see if I understand you - is what you're saying . . . . .?" Or you rephrase or repeat something the client said and add the tag, "Does that sound right?" or "Did I understand you correctly?"

These types of questions help you clarify points and assure both of you that you are "on the same page". During the interview process, your questions will probably be a mixture of different types of questions, but the majority of your questions should be open-ended questions, the kind that encourage your client to talk.

THE GIVE AND TAKE PROCESS

Regard the whole process as a "give and take" exchange. The person asking the questions is always the person in charge, not the one answering questions. You want this time to be light and enjoyable for the client and to create a feeling of having a conversation. Do not handle it in such a way that the client feels as if she is being interrogated. So periodically, intersperse questions with information, comments and occasionally an example of what you've done for someone else that may relate to the topic. Keep those examples to a minimum, however. If this is done very sparsely - a comment here, a similar experience there - the client will feel confident about your experience and expertise, even though in the beginning you might have no other experience than what you've done in your own home. That's why it's an excellent idea to see immediately if you can "practice" on some homes of relatives or close friends (for free, of course). Then in the interview process (or over the phone before you get the appointment), you can mention some of the improvements you've given others. You don't need to call them "clients". Refer to the "beach home I rearranged last week" or "the senior citizen's apartment I completed recently" or such. If the client or prospect assumes these were actual clients, let them assume what they wish. You haven't claimed them to be clients, but the work you did is just as legitimate when done FREE for a relative or friend as it is when you have been paid for it.

If you have a good memory, you're really not going to need to take notes. But in the beginning when I first started, I was worried that I would forget (and a little overly worried about not looking professional enough), that I prepared in advance a question form and I methodically went through my form and my questions were already printed on the form so that I wouldn't forget what to ask.

Do this if you feel you need the support, but I think you'll soon find you don't need one and that it's much better to go through the interview process without a form, or even a note pad. This way you can keep your attention focused directly on your client. Eye contact is very important. The client needs you to look at her whenever she is talking. That is the best way for her to tell you are truly listening to what she is saying.

The Waiver Form and Payment Agreement

THE WAIVER FORM - Now this is the tricky part. You're probably going to be tempted to skip this part but I advise you to do it. For many years now, our society has become a "sue happy" society. People will sue other people at the drop of a hat. And there is an erroneous but common conception that they can sue you for things not involving any kind of negligence on your part - just their aggravation.

This has never happened to me, and hopefully it will never happen to you, but you need to recognize that in this day and age, anything is possible.

This is why I ask, no insist, that all my clients sign a Liability Waiver. It doesn't have to be long and full of legal jargon, but it should cover the subject adequately and assist you in protecting yourself.

While I am certainly not an attorney, nor do I claim that the following waiver statement will totally protect you in the event you have a problem of this nature (and I do recommend that you speak with an attorney for all legal issues pertaining to your business), here is the one I currently use.

This is just a brief statement on a sheet of paper that I ask my clients to sign at this point. Every state has different laws. See a local attorney. I am not in the business of providing legal or accounting advice and shall not be responsible in any way for the wording in any document you use in your business, not any claims or representations you make. I do highly recommend the services of having a membership with LegalShield, not only to protect you and your business, but your family too. Memberships are extremely affordable and I have benefitted from mine so many times each year I cannot tell you. If just for the peace of mind, it's worth having. To speak with an independent associate, please write to davefahs@earthlink.net. He'll be more than happy to explain your many options to help you best protect yourself. Then you can have an attorney specialist in your state help you by reviewing all documents you wish to use in your business free with your membership. They will advise you on unlimited issues by phone with a home based business rider added to your personal membership.

Most people will be agreeable to signing the Waiver but you may encounter someone every once in a while that needs reassurance. Up until this point they probably haven't given a thought to whether anything might get damaged or broken in the process, and suddenly now they become apprehensive. Try to verbally reassure them about how careful you always try to be, that you've never had a problem in the past (hopefully you haven't), but then let them know that this is company policy and that all your previous clients have been agreeable and have signed the Waiver. They will probably sign it at this point.

If you are unlucky enough to get someone who refuses to sign the Waiver, then you have a choice. You can say to them that they will have to do all of the moving of the furniture and accessories themselves and you will simply direct where it should go; or you can say you can not take the job and leave; or because it is your business and you must decide what risks you are willing to take, you could dismiss the Waiver and do the job anyway. I advise against the latter choice, but it is really up to you.

PAYMENT AGREEMENT FORM - Once the Waiver is signed, you should also bring out a Payment Agreement Form that you have prepared in advance which states the nature of the financial agreement between the two of you. If you are charging a flat fee, the amount should be stated on the form. If an hourly fee, the anticipated time involved and the hourly rate should be clearly defined. Some consultants charge a base minimum figure and then add an hourly rate if the project takes longer than a specified time. Whatever agreement you have already made with the client, the form should give you a place to indicate what the charges will be, which room you are rearranging, the address of the location, the date, and any other particulars you feel will clearly describe what you have been hired to perform.

Construct a form that covers every area you can think of, because whoever draws up the agreement in writing (in this case you and your company), that is the party that is held responsible for any ambiguities that might arise later. I have operated for years with no written contract whatsoever and never had a problem. But times are clearly changing, and if you've ever watched any court TV shows like the People's Court, Judge Judy or any of the rest, you quickly see how much better it is to have all your business agreements in writing. They don't have to be complex and shouldn't intimidate the client, after all you're only going to be moving some furniture and accessories. But they should adequately cover the basics of what you have agreed to do and how much the client will pay you for that service.

Not only will the written agreement protect you, in case a client ever refuses to pay you at the end (because you always do the service first and get paid at the end), but there is something in a written document that silently conveys to the other party that the terms are "non negotiable". It also shows you to be a professional business person when you have the appropriate forms to cover every stage of the process.

I advise dealing with the Payment Agreement Form AFTER the Waiver of Liability. The majority of concern will happen over the Waiver and not the service fee because the service fee has already been established and agreed upon before you scheduled the appointment. Dealing with the payment form at this point is merely a formality and will also shift the client's attention away from the Waiver right when you want a focus shift to take place. It's not mandatory, but it is considered good business to have the client sign an agreement of what the charges for the service will be and their agreement to that dollar figure. While I don't always take my own advice, believe me when I say, it's a prudent policy to follow.

Taking the "Before" Pictures

Once you have completed the interview process and your Liability Waiver and Payment Agreement are signed, you are ready to begin. If you have not taken your "before" pictures, now is the time to get out your camera and do that. Explain to the client that you always like to take "before" pictures so that you will have a reference later for your records. If you plan to use the pictures as "before and after" examples on your web site or in your literature (which I do all the time), you might also mention that you use the photos to give examples of your work to other prospective clients and add, "if that's ok with you". I've never had a client say it wasn't ok. In case it should be a problem in the future, you can always refer back to this brief conversation confirming that you did get the client's permission to use the photographs later. Be sure to mention you will not be using their name or address unless they give written permission.

Now let's cover how to take the "before" pictures. You want to take an adequate supply of pictures because you might not know how they will come out unless you use a digital camera. Most pictures have a tendency to come out too dark, at least for me, but then I'm no camera whiz. My camera of preference is the Olympus C-7070 wide angle digital camera. I've had it for a while and don't know if it is still available. No doubt there is a newer model out now. I love the wide angle for taking my portfolio pictures because you'll soon discover that you'll want to take as wide a shot as possible. Many rooms are small and you can't get back far enough to get a wide shot. A wide angle lens is very helpful. You want to do this part as quickly as possible, but take as many "before" shots as you can because once you start working it's too late to get any more "before" shots.

I try to take a picture of every wall in the room from the opposite side of the room. I also try to stand in every corner of the room and get a shot or two of the opposite corner. With a wide angle lens, it's pretty easy to get two complete walls in your shot (assuming the room is large enough). When you do this, your camera is going to pick up parts of two walls. You want to pay particular attention to getting a shot of the parts of the room which look the worst. You want there to be as much difference in your *before* shots from your *after* shots. It is the dramatic difference between the before and after that will have the greatest impact on future clients.

If you see smaller sections of the room that need improvement (the top of a desk or table, a shelf unit or such), take close up shots of those areas. Remember what areas you took pictures of as best you can because you're going to want to try to show those areas again in the *after* shots and how you improved the appearance of that desk, table or shelf unit, etc.

If you feel you have time, you might want to try to take both digital and traditional photographs. But be sensitive to your client. If she is busily doing something else, like cleaning or fussing with kids, etc. then you have more time, but if she's standing around and waiting on you, then get this part over as soon as possible.

When done, put your camera(s) back with your tools but on top of your case as a reminder to take the "after" pictures when the job is complete. It would be unfortunate to have to ask a client if you can come back to get your after pictures. These are critical to the on-going success of your business because, it's really true, a picture **is** worth a thousand words. When prospects see what you have accomplished for other homeowners, they are much more apt to hire you to solve their decorating problems. Words are not as critical when you have pictures speaking for you.

Taking Measurements

In the beginning, you will probably want to take some measurements. I usually don't, but then I've been doing this a long time. But I still take measurements of the room and draw out a quick sketch from time to time, particularly when I see that the configuration of the room and the architectural elements in the room are complex and need some extra thought. This gives me time to think and weigh my options quietly without the client feeling as if I am wasting time.

So let's assume you're going to take measurements. It's really helpful if you have some 1/4" graph paper to use. In the design business, 1/4" is always equal to one foot. So if the room measures 20 feet in one direction you can easily draw a line 20 boxes long on your graph paper. Indicate where there are breaks in the wall, such as doorways, windows or other architectural elements (thermostats, light switches, etc.).

Continue on around the room until you have drawn all four walls and so you have a good feeling for the basic architecture of the room and the amount of space you have to work with.

This way you will easily be able to identify the natural traffic patterns that the room dictates. You could draw arrows on your layout at this point showing the traffic patterns. You'll need to make sure there is access to the windows and doors at all times.

TRAFFIC PATTERNS

Here are some general rules for traffic patterns. You always want to make sure you have enough clearance so that the room is both functional and safe:

- o For major traffic paths, leave four to six feet open.
- o For minor traffic paths, leave one foot-four inches to four feet open.
- o To have foot room between seating area and the edge of the coffee table, leave at least one foot.
- o For foot and leg room in front of a chair or sofa, leave 1-1/2 feet to 2-1/2 feet open.
- o Leave three feet open in front of a piano chair or bench.
- o For occupied chairs, allow two feet per person left open.
- o Leave 2 feet to three feet as the open space to get into chairs.
- o Leave 1-1/2 feet to two feet of open traffic path around the table and occupied chairs.

- o For making a bed, leave 1-1/2 to 2-1/2 feet open around a bed.
- o Between twin beds, leave a traffic path of between 1-1/2 feet to 2-1/3 feet open.
- o In front of dressers, leave at least three feet of walk space to allow you to open the drawers.

After you have the room's measurements and you have noted the traffic flow for the room, I advise you to take the measurements of the major pieces of furniture in the room that will be staying. At this point, if your client has mentioned the removal of any of the furniture in the room and you know you are not going to be using it, it would be a good idea to move it out of the room immediately to allow more space to work with what remains.

The only measurements you will really need to take are the width and depth. Occasionally you might need to measure the height of something. Jot down on your paperwork the name of the furniture and it's measurements. As you begin to work and try to decide if a certain piece will fit a certain place, your measurements will all be readily available and you should double check them first before moving something, particularly if it is heavy or expensive or particularly cherished by the client.

Chapter Seven

Rearranging the Room

Assessing the Room

At this point I always tell the client that I am going to take a little time to study the room and weigh the different options I might be thinking about. You see, most rooms can be successfully arranged in more than one way, so you need to think of different options and ultimately select the one that works best for the client based on the activities of the room and other aspects you gleaned in the interview process.

I also explain to my client that, while I am going to be using standard design concepts to rearrange the room, if there is anything I do that they simply don't understand or feel uncomfortable about, they should feel free to express those feelings to me immediately. I stress that I want them to be happy in the end and that I will be looking to them throughout the whole process to make sure they are comfortable with what I am doing. This is a very important step. Some people will be automatically bold in telling you what they like or don't like. Others will be painfully shy. If you give them permission up front to express their feelings, assuring them that they will not offend you in any way, you will lift and remove all that anxiety as the process begins and continues.

NOTE: More often than not, you'll probably be faced with the challenge of arranging a room that has a natural architectural focal point (such as a fireplace or large bay window) or where the main activity for the room is the television set or entertainment center. People generally watch more TV than enjoy a fire in the fireplace, so I'll say right now very emphatically, when the room is used for watching TV you need to move the TV as close to the natural focal point as possible, without exception.

Unless the room is very large and there is sufficient room and furniture to allow a separate area for watching TV, you're going to want and need to combine the TV with the focal point so that the main seating arrangement can allow your clients to enjoy both at the same time. This is very, very important.

The Main Seating Arrangement

Having said that, and assuming that you have either already been trained or are in the process of getting trained in the area of arrangement design, it is common sense to begin your room rearrangement with the main seating arrangement. If you are dealing with a living room or family room, there is probably going to be a sofa in the room. Apart from a TV or entertainment center that needs to be moved so that it is nearby any other element in the room that commands attention as a focal point, the sofa will become the anchor for the room and will literally dictate where all the rest of the furniture will be placed.

So if there is a TV, let's hope that it is already in the ideal place or can be moved to the ideal place without much problem. I have often found that the TV is situated in the wrong place in the room and the owner is reluctant to move it because it is hooked up to the outside antenna or cable and a complicated adjustment would need to be made to accommodate it elsewhere in the room. Whenever this situation arises, it doesn't mean the situation is hopeless, but it does make the arrangement choices more limited and more complicated.

Under no circumstances should you become involved in moving cables or doing any electronic work. If the client is willing for the TV to be moved, under the condition that they will have another licensed professional make any changes to the homes wiring that may be necessary, then go ahead and work with the client to move the TV to a more useful place. Otherwise, try to work with it just where it is, even if it is not the ideal place. Definitely explain all of this to the client, however, no matter which way it ends up.

Of all of the homes I have personally rearranged, it is the TV/Entertainment Center that has caused the most difficulty in getting the room properly rearranged. But you can only accomplish what your client will allow you to accomplish. And if, in the end, the arrangement has been compromised because you could not move the TV to a better location, I advise you to make a notation of this on the final invoice. That way, if there should ever be any friction regarding the service you provided, you have noted any situation that made it impossible for you to achieve what you would have hoped to do and that the client knew this and accepted this dilemma as being something that was outside your ability to control.

Some clients just don't want to be hassled with changing, extending or doing anything to the cords and cables for their electronic equipment. It's their home. Let them have their way and work around the situation as best you can. The process is very easy if there is only one major focal point in the room such as you see here. You can see here that the seating arrangement draws your eye directly to the room's focal point and the whole look and feel of the room is cohesive and inviting.

The Secondary Arrangement

Once the main seating arrangement is in place, look for ways to start to accommodate the other wishes your client has expressed to you for the room in your interview. In this photo there are two types of secondary seating, but they are clearly not placed properly and the room does not feel good. A re-designer's job is to solve these types of problems by providing a great arrangement that is functional as well as beautiful. This may or may not be possible given the furniture you have to work with and it also may or may not be possible given the space that is still available. But when you know what you're doing, a solution should be possible. I've never had a room stump me yet.

In most cases you're going to want your main seating arrangement to be no more than about 8 feet from the focal point. So unless the room is unusually small, there should be plenty of room left for other interesting furnishings. Consider a secondary seating arrangement, like a chair with a small table and lamp. Perhaps a desk unit with a chair. Perhaps a grouping of plants.

If at all possible, work to include as many areas for the general activities of the room and you will delight your client. I have found that most clients never think beyond the main seating arrangement, so here is one of the areas of the arrangement that you will really be able to surprise them and delight them at the same time.

Other Furniture

Once you have placed the main seating arrangement and tried your best to also accommodate areas in the room for other activities beyond what is typically done in the main seating area, then look at all the other furniture that either must stay in the room or that you would like to pull into the room to make it all work.

Typically this will involve some case goods, not counting the TV and/or entertainment center. You may have shelf units, chests, a desk, a bookcase, floor lamps and so forth that now need to be placed.

The whole goal at this point is to look for ways to balance the room. This can best be done by a good distribution of the furniture throughout the room. You want to avoid have one side of the room heavily laden with furniture while the opposite side has little to none.

You also want to avoid creating a roller-coaster look in the room, where there are huge differences between the heights of one piece of furniture compared to another piece placed next to it. The heights of the furniture should move up or down in gradual increments. It's much more pleasing to the eye.

You're also going to need to check the color balance in the room. This is dealt with in more detail in our design training. The various colors in the room, from the lights to the darks, need to be well distributed throughout the room to achieve the best balance. We also cover specifics on how to incorporate the natural and man-made lighting.

So it may start to get tricky at this point. Your job as an arrangement consultant is to make sure you have incorporated all of these elements together into a cohesive unit: balance, rhythm, color distribution, height distribution, focal points, traffic patterns, lighting, electronic needs, the room's activities. When you have done this, you will have succeeded.

I will be the first to say you will meet all of these standards with greater or lesser success. Some rooms will just "come together" instantly. Other rooms are going to be a real challenge. Every room is different. Every room presents it's own unique personality and dilemmas. That's what makes it fun and creative. And that's why your client can't do it herself and that's why you are in business.

Placing the Accessories

Do not start placing any accessories until all of the furniture is in place. Even veteran arrangers make additional adjustments with the furniture as they go along. There are many times that I just don't know if I'm going to be happy with a particular arrangement until I try it. There are also times when I've convinced myself that putting something in a particular place just isn't going to work. Then I move it there later and discover that it looks perfect in that place. Therefore be flexible.

So you really want to be sure that the furniture is just where you want it first before taking the time and effort to start arranging the art and other accessories.

But when you are ready for this stage, start with the lighting. Make sure that the lighting is well distributed and put in places where it will be functional and not create any hazardous conditions. In other words, you don't want to put a lamp where the cord might trip someone, yet you want to provide adequate lighting for people using the room. These are very important elements to think through carefully before you ever place the main seating arrangement.

By the time you reach the stage for accessories, you should have been receiving some solid positive feedback from your client. If you have not, then you need to find out if they are not satisfied with the progress at this stage. If they are not happy, you need to find out why. There's little point in progressing if your client hates what they see at this stage.

Assuming you have a happy client at this point, very carefully begin bringing the accessories back into the room and placing them. I have laid out several chapters in other eBooks or books that cover the proper placement of art and accessories so I am not going to delve into it here other than to say that the accessories and art are the real personality of any room. That's why they are so important.

Remember that there may be accessories your client has in other rooms that you can use. There may be accessories out in their garage, stored in boxes. So if you don't find what you need, be sure and communicate all of your ideas and wishes to your client. She is the only person who knows the full extent of what she has for you to consider using.

Handling of Client's Possessions

Before you move anything, you need to survey the room and look for any and all potential hazards that might be present. Hazards? Yes, things like small toys, slippery rugs, breakable accessories in precarious places, cords and other things you could trip over and such. Remove all such things immediately.

Even though you have a signed Waiver safely tucked in your case, you always want to take the greatest of care whenever handling someone else's property and treasures. Something might look old and beat up to you, but it could be a family heirloom, for all you know. Something might look very durable and in reality it is not. A sofa could have a broken leg that you cannot see. If the client has not already removed the most breakable objects from the room, have them do so at this point. It's better if they remove these things than if you do. Believe me, you won't have them arguing the point with you since they have signed the Waiver.

This is one reason why I charge a flat rate. I have done it long enough to know what kind of time frame I am most likely to incur and I make sure I've allowed enough time and charged accordingly for that time. When a client knows they are paying a flat rate, no matter how long it takes, they will not be pushing you to move quickly. You will not be pushing yourself either. When neither one of you is unduly concerned about the time factor, you will proceed more cautiously, which will lessen the likelihood of an accident. You definitely don't want any accidents to take place - not by you nor by your client. It can be guaranteed to ruin the day for both of you.

So take your time. Be as careful as you can be. And enjoy the creative part of the project which you are now about to enjoy.

Advising Your Client on Style

Does your client have a specific style that she is decorating in? Not sure? Let me help you break it down into easy segments. Here are some reminders in that area:

- Formal
- Conventional
- Modern
- Serene
- Dignified
- Simple
- Graceful
- Quaint

- Informal
- Unconventional
- Traditional
- Exhilarating
- Casual
- Cluttered
- Plain
- Sophisticated

You should note the style or combinations that the client has in the home, make suggestions on how the style can be enhanced further. You can also use this terminology to reinforce your client's taste and the direction you see them moving in as they continue to decorate the room or the home. This list gives you talking points to help you understand their goals and give more specific direction.

- Elegant
- Conservative
- Flamboyant
- Ordinary
- Dull
- Youthful
- Playful
- Luxurious

- Amusing
- Grandiose
- Strong
- Bold
- Graceful
- Offbeat
- Plain
- Ostentatious
- Amusing

- Dramatic
- Sedate
- Common
- Whimsical
- Opulent
- Powerful
- Understated Elegant
- Understated Casual

Goals of Good Interior Design

UTILITY - Your first goal should be *utility*. This means that the space you design should be effective and serve the primary purpose of the space. Your rooms should be designed to be useful, comfortable and efficient. But don't carry it overboard. Being too efficient can also be boring and cold. Make the usefulness of a room your primary goal, but don't make it the only goal.

ECONOMICAL - Your second goal should be *economy*. I'm not just referring to your client's budget, but to the saving of human resources, materials and the environment. For an example, a gourmet cook will want a totally efficient, large kitchen. I, myself, hate to cook, so I get by with a small kitchen that has low maintenance.

Instead of rushing out to buy a new gadget when an old one needs repair, tell your client to conserve and get the old one fixed. Many times they are made better anyway. Make an overall plan of your client's needs, so that they don't wind up making costly mistakes and buy unneeded items.

You can also conserve within the environment, not just for the sake of ecology, but for budgeting as well. Example: wooden objects have a long life generally speaking and can be refinished many times. When discarded, they will be absorbed back into the environment, whereas plastic or metal will not. Give old objects new life by repairing them, fixing them up and giving them a new purpose. Use your imagination.

BEAUTY - Ahhh, we all want things to be beautiful. Beauty enriches the senses, lifts the spirit and gives pleasure to the eye. It is personal. It is subjective. It expresses your taste. Always seek ways to make your home more inviting and pleasing to the eye. Sometimes it means adding something more. Sometimes it means reducing what you have. Seek beauty as a third goal. Remember, that just because a client has something in a room when you arrive, it does not have to remain in the room necessarily.

CHARACTER - How much time, money and effort you are willing to invest will dictate how personalized your client's home becomes. The client can gut their space and rebuild it according to their specifications. Or they can simply throw on a fresh coat of paint to an existing element. It's totally up to them.

Your ability to create character in their home will surface naturally. It is an extension of them, and that's the way it should be. Even if they do nothing, that is still an extension of them, their family and their lifestyle. Make it their special and unique space. Give it their personality. Be daring.

CLIMATE - Where a client lives is going to factor into your decisions. It will affect the materials they choose, the colors, the textures, the surfaces, the complexity. For instance, in a warm or hot climate, they'll want to choose "cool" colors, simple and uncluttered spaces that make them feel cooler. However, in a cold, damp climate, they'll be opting for warmth and feeling snug. So you'll most likely be looking at warm colors, plush carpeting and rich woods, with lots of furnishings to make them feel warm and comfortable.

LOCATION - A high rise condominium with a panoramic view of the city will most certainly affect your decisions as well as theirs regarding materials compared to a country home nestled in trees by the side of a lake.

MOBILITY - I've lived in my home for nearly 30 years and don't plan to move. Therefore my decisions regarding decorating will be very different from someone who doesn't plan to stay in one place very long. Whether you anticipate a relocation, a divorce, to turn a quick profit in a booming real estate market, or whether you just know you'll want something bigger and better in the near future, you're going to be affected by those goals and anticipations in ways I won't need to consider. Plan accordingly.

HOUSEHOLD - Your client's age and the age of their family are also considerations in your decision-making. Don't just plan their home for today, but keep the future in mind too.

Remember that their little ones are people too, and plan for their comfort and function as well. Keep everyone's privacy issues as a factor and remember how each member of the family interacts with the others. Allow everyone to have a private space where they can express their own individual personality.

LIFESTYLE - Another major consideration in decorating their home is their lifestyle. Are they a single person, spending most of their time away? Do they have a large family that likes to spend a lot of time at home? How much do they entertain? How large are their parties? Do they work from their home? These and many more lifestyle considerations should be taken into account before you arrange a home, and certainly when they are adding more furnishings to the home.

PSYCHOLOGY - Are they claustrophobic? Do they feel confined in small spaces, anxious? Does anyone in their family feel that way? Are they agoraphobic, overwhelmed in a large, open space? Is anyone in their family that way? An agoraphobic person needs a snug, smaller space to feel safe. The claustrophobic needs just the opposite. Rooms that will be used heavily by many members of the household should be larger, with higher ceilings and openness. Private spaces should be smaller with lower ceilings and fewer windows. Arrange their furnishings in the home to fit the psychological makeup of their family.

All in all, your goals should be to create a beautiful environment that is totally functional for the family that lives in the space.

Getting Client's Feedback

Through the process of rearranging your client's furnishings, you should be doing three things:

1) Finding ways to continually affirm your client on their choices of furnishings and accessories, making them feel supported and appreciated;

2) Explaining what you are doing and why, enlisting their help so they feel a part of the process;

3) Periodically checking with them to see if they feel comfortable with the changes you are making, asking for their input as well.

If you have done all of these things simultaneously and effectively, you should complete the whole process with a very happy client. If you sense along the way that there is a problem and they are not voicing their concerns, readjust immediately so that the client is happy. After all, even though you are striving to give them the best possible arrangement, it's still their home and they still need to feel comfortable living there after you are gone.

Collecting the Fee

I will discuss a little later in the next chapter what you should charge, but for now this would be the point in your consultation where you would collect the fee that your client has already agreed to pay. I have never had problems collecting my fee at the end. Even when a client has admitted they had to "get used to the new arrangement", I have never had any one balk at paying the fee. I sincerely doubt you will either, particularly if you have bent over backwards to make sure they are happy and accomplished the project in a reasonable length of time.

Speaking about time, you should make sure before you begin just how much time the client has available. Many times they will have some other appointment to go to later in the day, or for some reason need you to be done by a certain time. Always make sure you know how much time you have and keep track of the time as you go.

When I have completed the project, most clients are immediately going for their wallets to pay the fee. However, if they don't bring it up, I simply pull out my invoice and other forms, and I never even have to bring the subject up. Be sure to have some official invoices printed up, either on your home computer or at a print shop, because you want to look professional at all times. Never give a client a little store bought receipt from a booklet you got at the office supply store with your name stamped on it at the top. This is not going to gain you any respect. You're a professional consultant, not a day laborer.

Have the amount of the consultation written on the invoice, along with the client's name, address and phone, and email address (assuming they have one). If they pay you by check, record the check amount and the check number on the invoice. Give the client a copy of the invoice and retain one for your own records. If you receive cash, note that it was cash and write the amount given to you on the invoice before you give them a copy. Make all notations on the invoice in INK.

If I am ever given cash, I also place my initials by the amount given to me and request that the client initial the amount as well. This way, should there ever be problems arise, you both have stipulated to the exact amount of cash you received.

Never leave without getting paid! Never let a client "con" you into letting them pay you later, write you a post-dated check, or promise to send you a check in the mail. None of this! I've never had a client try it, but there can always be a first time. So I just want to go on record and tell you that you should never accept any terms other than payment on demand in full at the completion of the consultation.

The Referral and Testimonial Form

Now, this is the perfect and the only perfect time to ask for a brief testimonial (in writing) and one or two referrals. If you think you can call them back later to get this, or send them something in the mail to fill and return to you, you will most likely get nothing at all.

You must make the testimonial and referral gathering a part of the payment process. I have found it effective to even mention at the time that I set the appointment, that I will come and do the rearrangement, after which I will give them an invoice for payment and ask them for a brief testimonial and a couple of referrals, since I build my business mostly by word of mouth. Be sure to add the "word of mouth" phrase. It definitely helps.

If you have let them know ahead of time that this is part of the final process, you should not have any problem getting them to sit down for a brief moment and fill out your request.

I have an official form that first asks for a testimonial. It should only take them a minute to give you a few sentences about how they feel about the service you have just rendered to them. Getting a testimonial is important because you can add it to your marketing materials and to your web site. New prospects are always interested in how other people have found your service to benefit them.

You might even ask them to comment on how they feel they have "benefited" from the consultation. Remember, people aren't going to hire you because they like you or even because they think you are good. They ARE going to hire you because they believe you have something to offer that will BENEFIT them.

Don't ask for a bunch of referrals. Give them a place on the same "form", below the testimonial, to give you the contact information of 2-3 people whom they know whom they feel would be interested in hearing about your service. Tell them that you're looking for people whose homes they have been in whom they feel would benefit by a rearrangement. They should be people who care about how their homes look. They should be people they feel would be able to afford the service if they were interested.

Assure them that you will simply make an offer to them and will not badger them in any way. Since your client has just experienced the professional manner in which you have conducted yourself with them, and have experienced first hand the benefits of what you can do, you should find it quite easy to get them to give you a name or two.

If they claim, after your explanation of the type of person you are looking for, someone with equally good taste, that they just don't know anyone to pass you on to, then there isn't too much you can do at that point. Thank them and give them some business cards and ask them to pass them on to anyone in the future they feel could benefit by hearing what you do. Then in a month, consider re-contacting them to see if they have thought of anyone since you left that might appreciate hearing about your service.

A wise entrepreneur will have several referral gathering systems in place. Referrals can be very powerful and sustain you in business if you constantly seek them and have procedures in place that help you remember to ask for them. You must constantly ASK for referrals. Most people will not remember you later. And even if they did, they often forget what they did with your contact information and couldn't pass you on if they wanted to. This is another reason why it is important to periodically make contact with past clients. It serves, not only as a reminder to them that you are still in business and eager to help people, but if they have misplaced or thrown out any previous literature from you, they now have your contact information handy again.

Try to have that Testimonial and Referral Form filled out by your client before you leave the consultation. If you don't, the likelihood of getting it later is slim to none.

Taking the "After" Pictures

While the client is busy making payment and filling out your Testimonial/Referral Form, you should go ahead and begin taking your "after" pictures. You don't want to stand or sit watching your client write on your form. It may make them nervous and a little irritated.

Besides you are done now and you want to wrap things up as soon as possible and let them begin enjoying their "new space". So take your digital or traditional camera and try to find angles to re-shoot the room that are as similar to the "before" shots as possible. This can be tricky.

You want to have pictures of the same walls as the "before" shots, but at the same time you also want to shoot the room from a point of view where the arrangement can be easily seen and from an angle where the arrangement looks best. So I suggest that you take as many pictures as you can, because you're not going to know until later, when you have both the "before" and "after" shots lined up together, which ones can be combined to give other people the best feeling for the re-design you were able to achieve for your client.

These pictures aren't just for your later enjoyment. These pictures are to be used effectively in your advertising and marketing strategies to prove to other prospects that you have indeed made a major, significant improvement on the overall ambience of the rooms you have re-designed. Your prospective clients in the future are going to carefully scrutinize these "before" and "after" pictures to see if you know what you're doing and to see if your rearrangement ideas are going to most likely be worth the consultation fee you are charging. If they cannot see the value in the photos, you will most likely not see an appointment arise.

It's hard for a lot of people to visualize what you might do for them. If they were able to visualize, most likely they would be doing it themselves and not considering your services in the first place. So while you want to wrap things up at this point, don't be in such a hurry that you fail to take good "after" pictures. Your business depends on this.

If you have a video camera, you might also want to take some video shots of the room before and after the consultation. Having a video tape of homes you have done could be very handy in your marketing efforts, particularly if you enjoy speaking in public or conducting seminars. This is also an option.

No matter what method you use, however, get plenty of distance shots and close ups. They will all be worth the effort and will definitely help you garner more clients.

Advising Clients on Making New Purchases

You're always going to have some clients who need to make other changes to their decor by buying additional furniture or accessories or changing out what they already own. I personally preferred not to try to sell new products to my clients, but you can do that if you want. For me, this seemed kind of moving in the direction of a conflict of interest. I always assured my clients that I would make suggestions and then they would be free to purchase whatever they might need in the future wherever they liked. But there's nothing wrong with making some careful recommendations to help them out.

Whether you try to service your client with new products or not, you should develop a good list of stores or web sites that you might give to your clients. After you receive payment and your testimonial and referral form is filled out, this would be a good time to hand them a list of recommended places where you know they can acquire quality furniture and accessories at an affordable price. You could even divide it up into styles or simply by category. It's just one more thing you can offer your client that is above and beyond what you promised. This will always end the consultation on a very pleasant note with your client full of delight.

Leaving Business Cards

Always carry a supply of business cards with you. Make sure you leave a few with all your clients at the end of a consultation. Stick cards in the mail with bills you pay that go to local addresses. You never know whose opening the mail on the other end that might be interested or able to pass your card along.

I know of an attorney who would eat at a restaurant and never fail to leave the restaurant without passing out his business card to every customer there. I've never been bold enough to do that, but it worked for him. Let's face it - you never know when you might need an attorney. The same is actually true for homes that need help - you just never know.

Some people leave business cards in mail boxes, on car windows, at door steps. I don't know how effective this would be, but if you're seriously low on funds to get the word out any other way, it is another option. One good client can pay for a huge supply of business cards. I would be wary of leaving anything larger. People get irritated at flyers, but it is a rare person who would get irritated by a business card.

I have received a huge assortment of business cards stuck on my door, laid on the cement in front of my home. Most get tossed in the trash, but I have kept some in a special drawer that are of interest to me. I do always look at the card. That is what you want to remember. I think I'm a pretty typical homeowner, so I consider doing the things that do not offend me and I do not do any marketing strategies that offend me. Again, do unto others what you would have them do unto you.

Make sure that the design of your business card is well done. Remember, people will judge your design ability by everything you put out there. If I see a designer whose card is messy and ill planned, it tells me right away everything I need to know. This is not the place to cut corners, so if you don't feel competent to create a really nice calling card, hire a professional to create one for you. The same thing is true for your letterhead, your envelopes, your invoices and the like. Your materials are an extension of you -- make sure they "speak" well of you.

The Thank You Note

After every consultation, make sure you send a personal thank you note to your client. You can do this so easily if you've signed up for the card sending system I highly recommend, which I wrote about earlier. That web address again is **www.sendoutcards.com**. This is very important and you wouldn't believe how many businesses fail in this area. It is especially important for a consultant to send thank you notes. It shows your professionalism, it's just common courtesy, and it gives you another opportunity to communicate anything you may have forgotten, communicate anything you have thought of since you left the home, and serves as a reminder of your services.

If you offer additional products or services, which I always advise, you should know that 80% of your business in the future will most likely come from past clients, if you stay in touch. They have already experienced your service once and trust you. So it's always much easier and less costly to sell additional products and services to your past clients than it is to find new clients.

At any rate, I invariably think of things I want to further suggest to my clients while I'm driving back to my office. So not only do they get a nice thank you card from me, but I slip in a letter with all of the other ideas I want to share with them at the same time. This is my way of giving them "more" than I promised. When you do that you are always remembered more favorably.

The thank you note is also a very appropriate place to remind them and reinforce how lovely you think their home is, what nice choices they have made in selecting furnishings and accessories, and how enjoyable it was for you to work hand in hand with them to achieve the final result. Make sure they feel part of the "team".

If there were any misunderstandings during the consultation, this is another opportunity you have to clarify your position and reassure them of your continued appreciation of them, not only as a client, but as a valued "friend".

Thank you notes are so rarely sent, this one activity can mean the difference between on-going referrals and future business and none at all. Even if it brought you no benefit at all, I would still advise you to send a thank you note. It's just something that well mannered service-oriented people should do.

Reminders of Your Other Services or Products

All too often we assume that people understand our businesses -- the full scope of our products and services. The fact of the matter is, people don't. They can't be expected to know what you really offer.

We are all people who are focused on our own worlds. What we think and do is largely only important to us. So don't neglect to make sure you inform your clients, in some way, about other products and services you have that might be of interest to them or someone they know. Contact them periodically over a few weeks or months. Construct a newsletter full of helpful tips and send that to them regularly.

This is called "spaced repetition". This is one of the founding principles of marketing. Get the message out repeatedly to the same market in some kind of spaced period of time. Most people need to be contacted by you in some form or another 9-27 times before they will "buy" what you are selling. It takes time to build a relationship of trust.

So don't lose heart and think that just because you got the message out one time and you didn't get the response you wanted that your efforts were in vain. It is one part of a much larger picture.

When you first meet someone, you don't go out for lunch immediately, as a rule. No, you usually get to know someone over time, and eventually as a closer relationship starts to build, then you possibly do lunch. Well, the same principle applies to your marketing in an even more important manner.

People want to do business with people they feel they know and trust. So all of your marketing efforts should have one goal in Get to know them! Let them get to know you! Help them to trust you and see you as an expert!

You get to know them by being interested, genuinely interested, in them. If you're with a prospect and you're doing all the talking, you're not going to get the "sale". People really only value the things they say, not what you say. So getting them to talk about themselves, their home, their family, their activities and so forth -- these are all ways in which you come to understand them and show them that you care about them first.

Letting them get to know you must follow in a slower process. Letting them get to know you can happen easily by slipping something into the conversation from time to time that genuinely applies to what the client is saying. Experienced consultants never have to officially notify people of their accomplishments. It is gently woven very carefully into their conversation as they are focused on listening and gathering information from other people. Experienced consultants usually find that at the end of discussing a client's wishes and needs, they never have to "present their case" at all. The client has already become familiar with their expertise and experience just from some brief examples woven into the consultant's responses to comments or questions that the client has.

HOW TO WIN FRIENDS AND INFLUENCE PEOPLE

I wholeheartedly recommend you get a copy of the popular bestseller, "How to Win Friends and Influence People" by Dale Carnegie. It is an excellent book and will serve you well whether you're in business for yourself, whether you work for someone else and whether or not you work at all. I guarantee that this book will be one of the very best marketing books you will ever read. It is out in paperback and runs about $6. Regardless of that, here, briefly, are some important concepts to remember and use. Building trust and relationship takes time.

- Develop keen "listening skills".
- Keep your own words to a minimum.
- Show pictures whenever possible.
- Remain positive and confident at all times.
- Don't brag.
- Give more than you promise and promise a lot.
- Back everything you promise by a risk free guarantee (more about this later).
- Thank them afterwards.
- Affirm them positively whenever genuinely possible.

These are just a few of the ways, in a nutshell, prospects will come to feel they "know" you and "trust" you. Then they will do business with you.

Chapter Eight

Charging for Your Services

Selecting the Right Fee

Is there a standard way to charge for your consulting services? No. It's really up to you and what the market will bear in your area. But here are some guidelines to help you decide what is best for you.

- Look at your marketing arena
- Decide what your time and experience are worth
- Research the market rate in your area
- Learn the psychology of charging for your services
- Learn what the ethics are

High end clients are accustomed to a fee-based structure for services they purchase. But in the middle range, you're going to find that some prospects are wary of paying anyone for their time and expertise. They are more accustomed to paying strictly for "products". You may have to tailor your fees for each client in order to optimize your success.

DECIDE WHAT YOUR ANNUAL INCOME SHOULD BE YOUR FIRST YEAR

I don't know what the income level should be in your region of the country. It does vary depending on where you live. Obviously, it's bound to be less in your first couple of years from what it has a potential to become.

So the first thing you need to do is be realistic of what you feel would be a reasonable income in your first year. Notice that I wrote "reasonable income". Don't try to overpay yourself; don't try to underpay yourself. Try to be as realistic as possible.

Take the figure you arrive at and divide it by 52 (the number of weeks in a year). Then divide that figure by 5 (days of the work-week) and divide that figure by 8 (number of working hours in a day). Now you will have the hourly rate of that initial figure.

Now triple that figure. This is the lowest figure you should charge.

Remember that your consulting rate must be a lot higher than the figure you initially got after the math, because of the overhead of your business and because you're not going to book every hour. Therefore, consider tripling the initial number you calculated.

Your fee should be close to the hourly fee that other designer's in your area charge, but only if you have fairly comparable expertise and experience. Remember that a prospect will always value the fee a traditional interior designer would charge more than someone who only rearranges.

BE COMFORTABLE WITH WHAT YOU CHARGE

You have to have a comfort zone. So the best rate is also the one you feel comfortable charging. In the beginning, you'll find yourself probably offering to work for less just to get some actual clients under your belt, get the photos and experience to build your marketing portfolio and confidence. You can always raise your fee as you go.

Keep this in mind. Decide what scale of client you really want to have. If your fees are too steep, some middle range clients won't be able to afford your services. On the other hand, if your fees are too low, the more discerning prospects, who really CAN afford your service, will think you are not sophisticated or experienced enough for them.

So it boils down to this: Make sure you have done a good job of showing your prospects all of the benefits they will receive for this somewhat "intangible" service. Charge the highest fee you feel you are worth; but be comfortable in what you charge.

You may have to test the market a bit before you settle into something consistent. Testing is also a good marketing habit to develop.

OFFER A BONUS OR SPECIAL PRICE FOR EXTRA ADDED VALUE

More and more often, people expect to get a little extra. Everyone likes to feel they have gotten a "deal" that others haven't received. So you might find it very beneficial to always offer a "special" rate. I do this very simply by saying, "I normally charge $_____ for my consultations in your area, but I'm running a special right now and I'll work with you for $_____ if you book the appointment today. Otherwise I'll have to charge my normal rate. When would be the best day for you?"

Offer a special rate but put a time limit on it. This will make the prospect happy but help you immensely to get them to book the appointment right then. The more time that passes between your conversation and a decision, the less likely you will be in booking this prospect at all.

It is human nature to put off making a decision. If they don't decide to hire you right then, they will probably not hire you. People just don't think things over and then act. So whatever you can say over the phone when you first discuss your consultation fee is most likely going to be the best (or only) chance you will have to convert this person into a client.

A "special fee" for acting immediately can make the difference.

ETHICS OF A CONSULTANT

Whatever you decide to charge, it is essential that you make *full disclosure to your client.* Your client has a right to know in advance exactly what you intend to charge and how much time you anticipate the consultation will take.

I give my client prospects a *special rate*, and I have a *minimum* I will accept before I book anyone. I tell them all of this up front.

I assure them that my charges will not exceed what I quote them, no matter how long it takes me to accomplish the project. Then I leave it to them to decide if they can afford my services. I want them to be able to make an informed decision. I don't like unhappy clients. They don't do me one bit of good. It's another reason why I don't like hourly rates. It adds an element of uncertainty into my client's thoughts and I don't want them to feel uneasy. I've been doing this business long enough to know before I walk out the door how long it's going to take me. You will get to that point yourself in time.

But I make sure that there is NEVER a secret kept from the client. This would be unethical. I wouldn't want it done to me. I don't do it to anyone else.

Quoting Your Fees

Never let a client suggest to you what they feel you should charge. No way. No one knows the value of what you bring to the equation except you. Never let others determine your worth. Never.

If someone were to suggest to me that I charge them the same or lower rate than they can find elsewhere, I tell them "Best wishes. Go there." Actually that has never happened to me. But that is what I would tell them if it did happen.

We're not talking about a *product* here. We're talking about the unique creativity, gained over time and trial that **you** bring to the project - not someone else. Don't ever let anyone compare you with any one else. What someone else charges is merely a loose guideline and bears little on your value in the final analysis.

I've never had a client try to define my worth, per se. But I have had them try to negotiate a better deal from time to time. One lady wanted me to travel an hour each way and didn't want to pay extra for my travel time. I held my ground and she ultimately agreed to my price. When I got to her home, I discovered she and her husband were quite wealthy (he was a top writer in the TV industry). How she had the nerve to challenge my rate was beyond me, but she did.

My time is worth money whether I'm sitting on the freeway or in their home. And in addition to that, I have wear and tear on my car and gasoline expense. So you have to factor all these aspects into the equation before you throw out a figure.

Not only do you have to weigh the distance, but the time of day you're going to be traveling. I live in Southern California where the traffic is horrendous during peak periods. If a client can only meet with me at a time when I know I will be in heavy traffic on my arrival or departure, I always factor this extra time into my quote. So should you.

Other Expenses

Here is a brief list of typical expenses you will definitely have to factor into your business. There will be others, no doubt, but you can definitely expect to pay for the following:

*   Phone
*   Health (optional), Liability and Auto insurances
*   Gasoline
*   Vehicle mileage
*   Tires

- Postage
- Printing
- Sample accessories (optional)
- Marketing materials
- Arrangement and moving tools
- Web site fees
- Advertising
- Record keeping materials
- Film and processing (unless you go digital)
- Office supplies
- Books, audio tapes, videos for on-going education
- Legal fees
- Bank fees
- Merchant account fees (optional)
- A computer (optional)
- Self employment taxes

When you stop to think of the massive costs involved in running most businesses, this business requires very little overhead. That's one of the reasons that make it so attractive. As I've stated earlier, there is also very little risk. I like that.

There is virtually no product to be inventoried. Nothing you have to send. You can literally hold all of your tools of the trade in a case. You can be mobile in minutes. You can make every minute count by listening to audio tapes while you travel that will help you market your business more effectively, or help you communicate better.

You work strictly by appointment, so if you have another job or a family, you can schedule your appointments when YOU are able to do them. Most of the time it doesn't feel like work; it's very rewarding. And you are paid a very nice fee for services. On top of that you'll probably meet some very nice and interesting people who will spark creativity within you that you didn't know you had. What can be better than that?

Your Professional Guarantee

Not all consultants offer a personal guarantee. I think you are foolish if you don't. But it's your call. I offer the ultimate guarantee! Why? Because people just won't take you up on it and it sure removes their perceived *risk* on the front end.

I offer to refund the entire consultation fee, up to 100%, if my client is not happy. And on top of that, I also insist on putting everything back exactly the way it was when I arrived. By tying the "put everything back" offer with the money back offer, you eliminate someone from asking for their money back while keeping the new arrangement. If you insist on putting everything back to where it was at the beginning, then if they want to keep the new arrangement without paying for it, they have to move it all BACK AGAIN to the previous arrangement themselves after you leave.

But trust me, you really don't have to worry about people taking advantage of the guarantee. I've never had a client ask for a dime back. I've never had a client ask me to put everything back the way it was. You won't either if you follow the advice I have already given on how to properly conduct your consultations.

So it's really not something to be concerned about. And since you really don't have to worry about it, why not make your guarantee really, really strong? You have everything to gain and nothing to lose - nothing.

If a worst case scenario happened, and you had a client ask for a refund AND for you to return everything to it's original place, the most you would be out is your **time** and **gasoline**. Would that be so bad? Of course not! You could recover from that instantly. So why not use it as a guarantee to lock in more clients?

This is called *risk reversal.* It's a very powerful marketing concept. You offer to take all of the risk upon yourself, leaving your clients with no risk whatsoever. It's much easier for them to say "Yes!" and schedule a consultation. And that is the goal. Besides, it's just good business.

Chapter Nine

Managing Your Business

When you are first starting out, survival is the goal. It is more important than success. If I equated it with a sport, survival is equivalent to staying on the field, playing the game, learning the rules and developing your skills and reputation.

So to help guide you in a start up process that is orderly and makes sense, here are some steps you might consider following:

- Decide on the legal structure of your business
- Select your business name
- If a fictitious name, register it and publish it in a legal newspaper
- Develop a solid business plan so you know where you're going
- Obtain the necessary permits and licenses required by your state and city
- Obtain your business insurance
- Open a business bank account
- Get a business telephone
- If not conducting your business from your home, acquire a business address
- Create your marketing materials
- Create a web site

All of this assumes you have the entrepreneurial skills, the design skills and the desire to dedicate yourself to building a consulting business of this nature.

Selecting Legal Structure

Your first decision here is to decide what legal form of business is best for you. There are three major types of businesses: a sole proprietorship where you (and your spouse, if you have one) own the business; a partnership (where you co-own the business with someone other than a spouse); or a corporation (where the stockholders own the business). A corporation provides the most write-offs and provides you with liability protection personally. Set it up where you are an employee of the corporation.

I do not provide legal consultation nor do I provide tax consultation. These decisions are best left to professionals and you should consult one if you are not sure what is best for you.

Each business form has its advantages and disadvantages. Some have to do with taxes; some have to do with the general operations of the business; some are control issues; some are liability issues and so forth.

Check at your local library for good source books. Here are a couple of suggestions: *Small Time Operator* by Bernard Kamaroff; *Running a One-Person Business* by Claude Whitmyer, Salli Rasberry and Michael Phillips.

Selecting a Business Name

Selecting a business name is an important part of your marketing strategy. The first thing you must decide is whether you wish to use your full name as part of your business name or whether you wish to use a DBA. DBA means "doing business as". It is a fictitious name and, therefore, must be registered legally.

Using your own name as your business name (such as Mary Smith's Decor Services) is all right. People will find it easy to remember your name. But in the future you may have hired other consultants or wish to sell the business. It is harder to sell the business and pass on the goodwill you have developed if you use your own name.

Clearly the name you pick should state in some way *what* your business is about and it should be easy to pronounce and easy to understand over the phone. Shy away from difficult spellings, names that can easily be confused with other businesses, names that may suggest your business does something it does not. In an age where we are overloaded with information, the easier your business name is to pronounce and remember, the better off you will be.

Know what your plans and dreams for the future are. You don't want to pick a name that is really rearrangement specific if you have definite plans to offer other services down the road. Think about the short term, but plan for the long term as well.

Check to see what the procedures are in your state or county for doing business under a fictitious name. In California, I have to first register the proposed name with a state government agency at the courthouse to make sure no other business with that name exists in the county. There is a fee for registering the name.

Once the name has been accepted by the court registrant, I must then advertise a statement in a legal newspaper for a period of 4 weeks. This legal notice states the names of the owners of the company, their residence addresses, the name and address of the business, and what type of business it is. Check your local phone book for the names of newspapers in your area that publish DBA statements. They charge a fee as well.

To make it simple, many newspapers will handle the registration of your DBA name and automatically publish the statement too for a fee of around $50. They can handle the whole process quickly and by computer. This is great because it eliminates a trip to the courthouse. You will want to have two extra names available just in case your first choice is not available. You can even do this online.

Once the DBA has been processed and the name approved and you have proof that you have submitted the name to a legal newspaper for publishing, you will be able to open a bank account in the name of your DBA. I venture that most States have similar requirements, but since they are not all likely to be the same, you should inquire first to make sure you have taken every step necessary to set up your business' name.

Business Licenses

There are several licenses that you will probably need.

CITY BUSINESS LICENSE

Not all cities require you to have a license for a home based business. You need to call your city hall to inquire about this. In my city I not only need to pay a yearly license fee, but I am required to keep my business limited to only one room in my home (and it cannot be my garage). I am also prevented from posting any signs about my business on my property and I cannot have any clients coming to my home.

Your city or town may have similar regulations so you need to find out first what those are, so that you are in compliance.

RESALE LICENSE

Not all consultants need to have a resale license. Generally you must charge tax on products that you sell. If you sell a service (such as your time and expertise) you do not need a resale license. To make sure of your requirements, however, you should check with your local State Board of Equalization.

In California, a consultant must charge sales tax on their consulting fees that are attached to the sale of a product. I have a resale license because I do far more than rearrangement services.

If you do get a sales tax license, you will be required to fill out quarterly reports and send in all sales tax collected each quarter. If your business is very small, they sometimes require a report only at the end of the year. It's best to check with a local accountant to make sure or talk directly with someone at the State Board.

There is usually a deposit that you are required to pay which the Board will hold for 3 years in a savings account to guarantee that you pay your taxes. This fee is in part based on the amount of sales you anticipate making in your first year, so if you are asked to speculate on how much business you will be doing, keep the figure low to reduce the fee you might have to pay.

FEDERAL IDENTIFICATION NUMBER

All businesses are required to identify themselves on forms and licenses by one of two numbers: either your Social Security Number (SSN) or a Federal Employer Identification Number (EIN).

If you decided to set your business up as a sole proprietorship, you will need your SSN until such time as you hire employees, form a corporation or form a partnership. At that point you will need to have an EIN. If you do not plan to have employees at the start, file Form SS-4 with the IRS. There is no fee. Do not file for an EIN until you know you're hiring employees, otherwise the IRS will automatically send you quarterly and a year-end payroll tax return that you must fill out even though you don't have any employees. Don't put yourself through that until or unless you have to.

A partnership or a corporation must have federal and/or state EIN numbers whether they have employees or not.

Payroll

If you do have employees, or you have started your business as a corporation and you are receiving a salary as an employee of the corporation, I recommend you hire a payroll service to handle the processing of all of the checks and reporting all of the payroll taxes to the appropriate governmental agencies.

Payroll is a time consuming and confusing task that is best left to the professionals to handle for you. Don't let yourself get bogged down with it. Your time and energy are going to be much better deployed in concentrating your focus on marketing your business and servicing clients.

Check your local phone book for a good accounting/payroll service with a competitive rate. It is money well spent. Be sure to shop around. There is quite a bit of difference in the rates of payroll services. Be sure you know what their services include and what they do not. A lot of banks recommend ADP for payroll. I found them to be overpriced for my area.

Mission Statement and Business Plan

Develop a mission statement for your business that is really specific. To really define it properly, write it down. In order to get where you want to go, you have to know in advance where you want to go, otherwise you're going to end up somewhere else.

You not only need to know where you want your business to go, you need to have a plan of how you're going to get where you want to go. It's wise to write all of this down, review it periodically, make necessary adjustments as you need to.

Think about the following elements that should be part of all this:

- the purpose of your business
- what special niche or target clients you want for your services
- what secondary markets there are for your business to fill
- how you will describe your service and promote it
- what the most compelling benefits are for your clients
- what is the most unique aspect that will separate you from your competitors (this is your unique selling proposition, USP)
- what back end products or services you could offer to your clients
- how you could utilize the internet to your advantage
- what policies and procedures you will put into place

Write everything down. Then pull it all together in a one or two page document that is as concise as you can make it. Develop a one sentence statement that really describes what you do and it's major benefit to your target market.

Start Up Budget

Your start up budget should be constructed as thoroughly as possible. The major reason most businesses fail is for lack of proper funding. Before making any major purchases, get quotes from two or three different sources. If you need to find an insurance broker, an attorney, or an accountant, shop around for the most qualified person at a reasonable rate.

If you have never been in business for yourself before, talk to your friends and relatives and ask for advice. Seek people who are successful, particularly if they own a business of their own. Most people will be happy to give you advice. They can steer you in the right direction for your locale to find the office supplies, equipment and other products you will need at the best prices.

Create a start up budget that is realistic. You will need to be well funded in the beginning to sustain you during the initial months.

Set up a budget that includes the following:

- *your start up costs:* initial investment, equipment needs: land phone and/or cell phone, typewriter, copier, fax machine, computer, answering machine or service, digital camera, props, calculator; installation costs of any equipment; your marketing materials, any remodeling or decorating expenses, licenses and permits, legal and accounting set up charges, your accounting system, business checks and a cash cushion.
- *your operating expenses for 3-months minimum:* your monthly draw or salary, outside services, rent (if not in your home), telephone, utilities, office supplies and equipment, advertising (yellow pages, etc), debt finance charges, maintenance supplies, taxes, legal and accounting services, insurance, answering service, promotional expenses, entertainment and travel, training/professional seminars or conferences, out of pocket expenses, auto expenses and miscellaneous expenses.

To break down your start-up costs further, consider the following:

- *Marketing Expenses:* Stationery and printing, business logo design, portfolio and briefcase, marketing materials, wardrobe
- *Business Organization Expenses:* accounting fees, decorating and remodeling costs, insurance, legal fees, license and permits, telephone installation, internet access costs
- *Operating Expenses of Your Office:* Office supplies, answering service, outside services, photocopying, maintenance supplies
- *Furniture and/or Equipment:* Desks, chairs, filing cabinets, typewriter, computer, telephone, fax, copy machine, tools of the trade
- *Other Expenses:* Gasoline, bridge tolls, auto repairs, client gifts, unexpected expenses

Creating Invoices

If you have a computer, your word processing program should come with some generic invoices and other types of forms that can be readily adapted for your usage. This is the route I would take. Do not pay a printer a costly fee to have NCR invoices printed off. You can do that kind of thing down the road when you are well established and doing a lot of invoicing on a regular basis.

But in the beginning, you're going to be spending most of your time getting set up and marketing your services and spreading the word. You can easily print off a few invoices as you need them. They will look every bit as professional.

If you don't have a computer to personalize your forms, then check with your local office supply company. Visual Organizer, Inc. was a company in the mid 1980's that published a book called, "Forms for Business". It was a compilation of all types of generic business forms. You only need to take a form, have your personal business information added to it, take it to a copy service, and have copies run off in any quantity you want.

Since most people have computers, or at least access to one, looking to your word processing software will still be your best source for ready made forms.

Record Keeping

It's not difficult to keep track of your consulting time. All of the information will be recorded on your invoices. Ask your local office supply store for samples of either manual recordkeeping books or accounting software which is easy to operate.

Keep all your receipts for every expense related to your business. These will become very important when you prepare your tax return. I have file cabinets to house all of my invoices and receipts. I create folders for the types of expenses that are repetitive, like my phone bill. For the receipts that are non repetitive, I have a miscellaneous folder that I use to store them in.

Bank Account

If you have elected to use a fictitious business name rather than your own personal name, you will need to file a Fictitious Name Statement and publish it in a legal newspaper before you can open a business checking account. You do not need to wait until the business has been published all four weeks to get your account, but you will probably have to prove that the process as been started.

The bank you choose is entirely up to you. I do highly recommend that you have a separate business account so that the revenue you generate is not co-mingled with your personal money. It's just good business to keep things separated, especially if you are ever audited by the IRS. You will not appear to be a professional business person if your business income is mixed in with private income, and this is something the IRS doesn't like at all.

It is also much more difficult to tell at any given point just how well you are doing in your business if the records for the business and the bank account are not separate entities. The checks you will write to pay expenses are not going to be seen by your clients, so don't feel that you need to have a certain kind of check. Keep your expenses as low as possible by any means possible. But before you order checks, know what type of bookkeeping system you will be using. Order your checks accordingly.

If you have hired an accountant, be sure to check to see what system he or she thinks would be best for you. Many of the convenient one-write check systems, that use a combination of checks and ledger, have checks that must be ordered directly from an office supply company rather than from your bank.

If your office is computerized, consider getting one of the simple bookkeeping systems that will save you a lot of time, such as Quicken. Many are designed for both PCs and Macs.

Pay all of your expenses with a business check or a business credit card, not your personal checks and credit cards. Should you ever get an audit by the IRS, the more organized and documented your business is, the easier the audit will go. For this reason, type the information on your checks instead of making them out by hand. It just gives a more professional image.

Business Telephone

Your telephone is your best friend. You cannot exist without this friend. As a consultant, you're going to be away from your phone often, hopefully, so you need an efficient system for receiving calls. At the very least you should have two incoming lines. Prospects and clients get really annoyed if they call and get a busy signal and you would be amazed how often you will get a phone call while you are on another line.

Use your secondary line for your outgoing calls, keeping your primary line open for incoming calls.

Decide whether you want to have an answering machine (which obviously lets people know that you have a home-based business) or a voice mail answering system or service (which makes you as a start up entrepreneur appear to be a more established owner.

ANSWERING MACHINE

If you choose an answering machine, make the message brief and current (unless you have one that allows your caller to press # to go directly to leaving you a message). The latter is nice since you can leave a more descriptive message about your services. The downside is that some people don't listen to the instruction about pressing # to bypass the longer message and they just hang up.

A sample short message might be:

"Hello, you've reached Mary Smith Decor Services. We're either on the phone or with a client. Your call is very important to us. Please leave a message of any length when you hear the electronic tone, and we will get back to you as soon as possible. Thank you."

This is all the information you need to give. Don't tell them to "have a great day" or give your itinerary for the day or week. Make sure your answering machine will allow them to leave a long message if they choose. It's very annoying to be cut off in the middle of a message. Most people won't call back to continue where they left off.

Do be diligent about checking your message and return phone calls in a timely manner.

ANSWERING SERVICE

I've personally never used an answering service. I'm sure there are good ones that will be reliable. Ask for references and be sure and call the references before you settle on one. Then periodically call yourself to see how the service is handling the calls. Check with your local phone service provider. They carry voice mail services that are very professional.

You may also opt to conduct business entirely with a cell phone. The more sophisticated services give you voice mail, as well as other nifty services. But be prepared to pay a lot more for your phone service this way.

Business Address

I highly recommend operating your business from home. First of all, it's really typical and not at all unusual for designers to have home based businesses. I doubt sincerely if any homeowner will care if your business is home based or not. I have operated a home based business from day one and the only thing that I cannot take advantage of is any "off the street" business I might pick up from some business signage. But then I don't have to pay out any high priced rent and my other expenses are much lower as well. I also don't have to sign any leases, pay out any deposits, provide insurance coverage that is mandated by a landlord, and so forth.

What I would avoid is using a post-office box as your address (like Mailboxes Etc). It not only does not look professional, but it could create doubt in the mind of your prospects about doing business with you. People want the reassurance that they can actually "find" you in person if they need to and that cannot be done if you are promoting a PO Box address. I don't know about other states, but in California if you use a mail box address, you have to designate your PMB number, which tells people instantly that it is a mail box address other than the US postal service.

So either select an actual business location and rent space or set up your business in your home. Always check with the local city or governmental offices to make sure you understand any zoning laws and license requirements.

If you just don't want to host the business in your home, you could also consider renting an office in a building where other small businesses join together to co-pay for the generic reception, telephone answering services and a conference room. These types of office set ups generally give you a nice, prestigious business address.

As a consultant, no matter what additional products and services you might choose to offer, you're really not going to have clients coming to your office. You're going to be going to their homes or offices. I have never found using my home address to be a problem. But it all boils down to what you are most comfortable setting up and what type of revenue you have to support yourself while you are building your business.

Marketing Materials

Once you have developed a marketing plan, you then need to create and design your marketing materials. With the vast majority of people owning or having access to computers and the internet, a well-designed web site will be the best marketing "material" you could ever create, in my opinion. First, it is just so inexpensive compared to traditional marketing materials, like a color brochure or color flyer. And it can be changed on a moment's notice.

If you don't have a web site, I would advise you to create strong marketing materials that you have stored on a diskette, zip disc or CD, which you could hand out or mail to a prospect. It's still much less expensive than paying a printer and because you're in the design business, you really do not want to create materials in black and white. You're just not going to impress anyone with anything less than full color.

If you don't know HTML, consider purchasing a pre-designed web site. They are kind of generic but will give you something pretty sharp visually. You just plug in the appropriate images and text using the web through FrontPage. A useful site with lots of templates you can purchase is FrontPageWorld.Com.

To make good decisions, people have to be able to visualize enjoying the benefits of your service. Here is the prime example of "a picture is worth a thousand words". Be generous with pictures or graphics.

Every time you want to feature a service or product, try to demonstrate it in some way. This is qualified, however, for a web site. Graphics take a long time to download and most people still have slow modems. On a web site try to keep your graphics to a minimum per page with files as small as possible.

Always strive to keep your materials current and in good condition. This is another good reason for having a web site to recommend to prospects. You can update a web site instantly if you know HTML or use a software program like FrontPage. You can't do that with a printed brochure, so the commitment to what you want on a brochure or flyer has to be images and text that are more generic and that you can "live with" for a longer period of time.

BROCHURES   If you do have a brochure printed up (or have a CD or disc), you could use them as an "interest sparker" before you have ever talked to a prospect, or once you have set an appointment, send one to reinforce the good and wise decision your new client has just made.

Here is a brief list of some of the ingredients you should consider including in your brochure. Keep the brochure short and to the point.

- Your business logo
- Brief statement describing your company: your business' reputation, your standards of quality, your credentials
- The range of services you provide: focus on the key benefits first, then the features
- Brief description of how you work and how you charge for services
- The scope of your business: the size, location and cities where you have worked
- Your staff and resources: your credentials and your experience that is relevant
- A list of some of your clients
- An encouragement for them to contact you or a "call to action"

Don't try to include everything. Use it as a "teaser", a door opener, a brief image or quality statement.

Keep your paragraphs short. Use 10 pt or larger type size. People over 40 cannot read small type. Don't use overly excessive feminine colors like pink or powder blue. Make it as classy as you can.

Don't overcompensate in your brochure because you feel your credentials aren't strong or you don't have many clients yet. Eventually your list of clients will speak for you anyway.

Don't include a history of your company. The prospect really doesn't care about your history. They just want to know who you are today and what you can do for them in the immediate future.

Don't include any long, boring, tedious resumes with data that is totally irrelevant to what you do now. As you write the copy, ask yourself this question after each sentence: "So what?" If you don't have a good answer, eliminate the statement or rewrite it.

Remove all design jargon. Write and talk as if the person was just a friend. Don't try to impress anyone with your verbiage. I once had an employee who had a great command of the English language and she took every opportunity to use as many 4 syllable words in the same sentence as she could. Her speech was belabored, boring and suggested she had a haughty attitude. She was unsuccessful and I had to let her go. Just be your everyday self. People will like you better and you'll get more work, I guarantee it.

Keep your copy from being overly promotional and boastful. Don't promise anything you can't deliver.

LETTERHEAD - Since your letterhead is something that a prospect may see first, or something a client will see last (if you use it for your thank you note), it is an extension of you, therefore important. Make it business-like. Don't use colored paper (unless a soft gray or tan), and avoid real flashy type. Try to give it a "corporate image".

BUSINESS CARD - This is your mini-brochure. If it stands out and incorporates a mention of your main service, people won't be quite as apt to throw it away or forget you. Keep your cards handy and give them out generously.

POSTCARDS - Postcards are an excellent way to advertise your services. They tend to stand out in someone's mail and are quick and easy to read – and they cost less than letters or brochures. We've designed some absolutely beautiful postcards you can get. They're generic so you can put your own label on the address side and let the postcard announce your business for you. For more information please visit Chapter Eighteen.

ORGANIZER/TOTE - To make you look absolutely classy and chic when you're out shopping for your client or for yourself, check out our Decorating Organizer/Tote. It's exquisite and so very well thought out. Wish I had invented it, but we do buy these straight from the manufacturer. You'll love it. Details in the last chapter of this book.

Business Insurance

When setting up your business insurance, I have found it helpful to work with a broker. Discuss the service you will be providing with your broker who should be most helpful in finding you the coverage you need at the best premium.

Most consultants need several types of insurance coverage: personal liability, general liability, disability coverage and automobile coverage. Coverage premiums will vary according to what you do, where you live and the types of places you will be entering to provide your services.

General liability covers all your office contents, equipment and business personal property while providing coverage in case someone is injured on your property. Discuss these issues with the broker because some coverage may already be adequately included in your homeowner's policy. Usually a standard homeowner's policy will not cover anything related to business, however. Your standard auto policy will usually not cover anything related to business either.

Disability insurance will cover you in case you are temporarily or permanently injured and are unable to work. Far more people wind up with a disability of some kind than are killed in accidents, so it might be very smart to consider insurance of this nature, particularly if you are relying on the income from this business as primary revenue for you and your family.

Again, I'm not an insurance agent or broker. Please discuss these issues with a professional that provides such services and then make an informed decision as to what is right for you and will fit into your business budget.

Business Automobile

As I just stated above, your personal automobile insurance will not cover any products inside that are used for business. So unless you also acquire business coverage, just know that you carry business tools, accessories or other products at your own risk.

If you use a vehicle for business that is solely used for business purposes, you can deduct all of the expenses for tax purposes, or you can choose to take a mileage deduction for the total miles driven in the year.

However, if you use the vehicle for both business and personal trips, then you can only deduct the portion of your expenses or mileage in your tax return that relates to business trips.

No matter what, save every receipt you get for expenses related to your automobile. In addition to that, buy an automobile record book from your office supply store that will help you register every trip you make. You will be able to enter the date, destination and purpose, your starting odometer reading and your ending reading. In case you get an audit from the IRS, you may need to produce this record of trips to prove you have a legitimate deduction.

Technically, you are not allowed to deduct mileage of your first trip of the day and your last trip of the day (it equates to "commuting" mileage). If you have a home based business, the first trip and the last trip would equate to the mileage of someone who goes to a particular place to work. If you visit the bank first (which is ideally close to home), that can be your commuting mileage "to work" and if you visit some other business close to home on your way back, the mileage from that business establishment to your home is considered your commuting mileage "from work". This is just a small tip of how to maximize your deductible mileage. It may not seem like much of a deal at first, but you'd be surprised how much it adds up over the course of a whole year.

Tax Preparation

This is such a vast subject and a very important one, that I advise you to consult a tax specialist right from the start. Having said that, let me then say that you want to really become focused on looking at every expense as a possible tax deduction. Get a clear understanding of what will be deductible and what will not.

But don't get so focused on the fact that something is tax deductible and spend, spend, spend. Ultimately it's still money out of your pocket, so use common sense and discernment before jumping into any expenses that are truly not mandatory. Little things can eat up your profit very quickly and then you might get discouraged.

Be as organized as you possibly can. Save all receipts and try to enter them in a bookkeeping system that is easy to use and understand. Consider hiring a tax specialist to prepare your tax returns, at least in the beginning, if you've never done a business tax return.

Sole proprietors will file a Schedule C along with their personal federal tax return. Corporations will have to file a separate corporate tax return. Partners will file their own tax returns based on their percentage of the business profit and the type of partnership set up.

Know what your profit and loss statement shows before the end of December so that you can pay off additional expenses before the end of the year, if you need to reduce your taxable income.

There are several excellent software programs that you can purchase that will assist you in filling out your tax returns, if you chose to do them yourself. H & R Block makes a good one called "Tax Cut" and there are others. These programs will not only help ensure that you deduct every expense you are entitled to deduct, but they also will carry forward all of the pertinent data from one year to another and this makes filing your tax returns a breeze, sort of. Doing taxes is never a breeze!

Resources
Excellent resources can be found at the end of the book. You can always visit my website to get more details on any of them.

Chapter Ten

Publicity and Advertising

Publicity and advertising are very closely related and often confused to mean the same thing. They both deal with how the public views your image. However, publicity and advertising are different. Publicity is generally exposure you are able to get for your business which you do not have to pay for: articles in the newspaper or magazines, interviews at radio or TV stations. Publicity is fantastic, not only because it is free and reaches a wide audience, but because it is viewed by the consumer as a *third party endorsement*. People tend not to view it as an advertisement and, therefore, put more credence in the information.

Advertising is more suspect because of the self-serving motives behind the ad and because there is a tendency to believe that claims by the advertiser are inflated or even bogus. People tend to take claims made through publicity as being fact and reliable. That's the power of *third party endorsement*, or at least the appearance of such.

Press Releases

Second only to word of mouth recommendations from clients, the best marketing tool for your business is a newspaper or magazine article featuring you or your services. It can be very persuasive.

People continue to be curious about what is written *about* others. Most people don't know that many of the articles that they read in newspapers or magazines were written by the person the article is featuring and not by a staff writer. They assume the latter. Impressions lodge in the reader's brain but they may not remember how or where they heard about you. The result is that a sense of familiarity with you arises long before they meet you or speak to you. And since confidence in you and your service is a necessary ingredient before they will do business with you, *third party endorsements* aid that process.

Whenever you have something new, or you are "tweaking" an older, traditional concept, the press should be interested. This is called "soft news". Whenever I send off press releases, I always write them as if someone had interviewed me. I use the third person pronouns, include quotes, and always include my contact information in some way in the first paragraph. I have found that media people like it when they don't have to write the article from scratch, and if they aren't going to print all of what I write, I certainly don't want my contact information to get edited out of the piece.

There are many good books on the subject of gaining publicity - web sites as well, where you can pick up free tips and strategies, download electronic books or whatever you need to help you effectively write newsworthy articles.

Always remember that a good article will answer the following questions in the first paragraph: who, what, where, when, why and should also have a headline that peaks a reader's curiosity. A compelling headline is vital because most people don't "read" articles - they skim headlines.

A new friend of mine who has a successful rearrangement business in Nashville, TN by the name of Teresa Truitt Weidner sent me some additional tips which I will share here and how she has successfully garnered substantial press coverage for her business in the year or two she has been doing redesign.

How to Do a Press Release

Here are some of Teresa's tips, together with some of mine, for preparing a Press Release.

1) Make sure that the information you are reporting is newsworthy. If you believe the information would interest you if it was about someone else, then it is newsworthy.

2) Get your contact information stated clearly and fully. Reporters and editors work on non-traditional schedules and don't have time to be searching for how to contact you. So be sure to include such information as: your name, address, business phone, fax, after hour numbers, your cell phone, pager and your web site, if you have one. Don't let your news release get trashed because they couldn't contact you.

3) Create a compelling headline that summarizes the newsworthy event you are announcing.

4) Don't hype your article. Avoid adjectives that are puffed up and fluff. Editors see right through that. Give them the facts and don't go on and on.

5) Be sure your press release is sent to the right department or editor whose readership or viewers are specifically interested in your type of product or service.

6) Use your business letterhead. It's always best to type it, double spaced, but if you can't then print it neatly. Make sure your spelling is correct.

7) At the top of the page, put the phrase "For Immediate Release" with your contact information below. This will tell an editor that they can use the release at any time they choose.

8) Make your headline in large, bold, and easy to read lettering. But don't make it so large that it is glaring. Don't use a fancy font. The type of lettering in this Primer is perfect and easy to read.

9) Begin your opening paragraph with the city and state of your business. Editors want to know where the article originated; this is called a "dateline".

10) Try to keep the news release to one page, but if you go over, center a "#" sign or the word "MORE" at the bottom of the first page so that it is obvious there is another page.

11) Do not go over two pages for best results.

12) On the second page, place the page number and the first two or three words of your headline in the upper left corner and repeat your contact information. Should your second page get separated from the first page, your contact information will still be in tact.

13) Don't split a paragraph in half with some copy on one page and the rest on another page. Re-space it so that complete paragraphs are all on one page.

14) At the end of the news release, let the editor know that it is the end by placing three "#" signs in a row, centered on the page. Example: # # #

Here is an Actual Approach to Try

"Hello,

I would be interested in providing a story or article for *NameofNewspaper*. I have had several articles in the *Competingnewspaper*. Please visit my website at: www.*nameofyoursite.com*.

I am also filming a segment for Talk of the Town on November 15.

I specialize in One Day Room Makeovers, Interior Redesign and Home Staging . . . I am a member of an association that has been featured on Oprah and HGTV.

Please call if there is an interest for an article."

Then put your contact information.

BIOGRAPHICAL INFORMATION AND PHOTOS

You should also create a one or two page biographical sheet on your self and your business. You send this out to media people when you are requesting them to do a feature article about you. Have available two black and white photos of yourself. The first should be a 5x7 head and shoulder shot. The other should be an 8x10 shot of you in someone's home, perhaps in the process of moving furniture. You can include one of these photographs with your press material whenever it is appropriate.

Remember, the real value of promotional articles is not so much when they appear or where they appear, but the reprints you will be able to use afterwards to send out to prospects or to other media people you want to interest. Press people are just as vulnerable as the general public. They will assume you are an authority in your field if you submit evidence of previous publicity about your self.

You can research publications at your local library in the *Gale Directory of Publications,* an annual guide to periodicals.

Thirty-Two Ways to Create Publicity News

1. Tie in with news events of the day.
2. Work with another publicity person.
3. Tie in with a newspaper or other medium on a mutual project.
4. Conduct a poll or survey.
5. Issue a report.
6. Arrange an interview with a celebrity.
7. Take part in a controversy.
8. Arrange for a testimonial.
9. Arrange a speech.
10. Make an analysis or prediction.
11. Form and announce names for committees.
12. Hold an election.
13. Announce an appointment.
14. Celebrate an anniversary.
15. Issue a summary of facts.
16. Tie in with a holiday.
17. Make a trip.
18. Present an award.
19. Hold a contest.
20. Pass a resolution.
21. Appear before public bodies.
22. Stage a special event.
23. Write a letter.
24. Release a letter you received.
25. Adapt national reports and surveys for local use.
26. Stage a debate.
27. Tie into a well-known week or day.
28. Honor an institution.
29. Organize a tour.
30. Inspect a project.
31. Issue a commendation.
32. Issue a protest.

From Wilcox, Ault and Agee, Public Relations: Strategies & Tactics, 3rd ed. (1992), p. 274. With permission.

Press Release Web Sites

Here are some web sites that you can visit if you are interested in having a Press Release submittal service help you reach a large audience. Please investigate their services carefully to make sure you understand what they offer and what they do not offer. Be wary of any one who promises your submissions are guaranteed. These services do not control editors and journalists.

Gebbie Press (www.gebbiepress.com)
PR Newswire (www.prnewswire.com)
The Paperboy (www.thepaperboy.com)
The MagazineBoy (www.themagazineboy.com)
Press Release Network (www.pressreleasenetwork.com)

Bacons Information
Oxbridge Media Finder (www.mediafinder.com)

Advertising

Advertising is probably never as effective as publicity, no matter what field you are in. It is particularly so for consultants, however. This is because when someone wants to find a consultant, they generally do not go to the yellow pages or to the newspaper or magazines to find one. They usually ask someone they know to advise them. For this reason, typical advertising is generally a waste of time and resources.

However, ads may be useful when you want to reach a special target audience. So if you are considering the use of traditional advertising methods, look for special interest magazines, such as House Beautiful or Better Homes and Gardens. But know that this form of advertising is very, very expensive and requires at least a two or three month lead time. That's a long time to wait for an ad to come out.

A small listing in the yellow pages where interior designers and decorators advertise is good, but a large ad will probably be a waste of money.

Word of Mouth

As I have stated earlier, word of mouth advertising and recommendations from clients who have benefited from your services is the most powerful and effective form of building any business, particularly that of a consultant. That is why it is so imperative that you learn and develop the habit of asking for referrals whenever possible and from as many people as possible.

Just as third party endorsements derived from publicity are beneficial to you, word of mouth from a third party endorsement is even more powerful. It is far more personal, as well. Be sure to ask all your clients for referrals. Do so immediately following your consultation, right there before you leave.

Follow up in your thank you note with another reminder or request for referrals.

In a month or two, consider sending your clients some additional information that will help them decorate their homes. It could be anything: an article you read that you think would be helpful; another suggestion for some other part of their home; a list of places to shop for unique accessories that would suit their taste and style; places to shop where they can get a bargain. It really doesn't matter what you send to them, it gives you an excuse to put your name and business in front of them. It shows you care about them *after* the consultation is over, not just at the time.

They may have met new people since you last had contact. They may have learned about someone new in the neighborhood or someone at work who has just moved. You want them to remember you favorably for as long as you remain in business. Always give them something that will benefit them and they will remain your ally. You never know when the phone will ring and someone will tell you that they received your name from a former client.

Most of the time when this happens, the earlier client will have already told this prospect how much the consultation cost and so you can be pretty sure that if you suggest the same price, the consultation fee will not be an issue. If it were, they would never have called you in the first place.

Try to develop at least 5 different referral gathering procedures and work them faithfully. It may take awhile, but give it a chance. What have you got to lose? And besides that, the best part is - it's practically or totally FREE. You can't beat the price, that's for sure.

Chapter Eleven

Strategies for Success

As I write this, the United States economic condition is pretty strained. In the past few years we have existed in the aftermath of the September 11 tragedies; then huge corporate bankruptcies and scandals. Times are very uncertain with the terrorist threat always looming in the background and an economic upheaval in housing, credit, stocks, currencies and insurance, not to mention job losses, crude oil prices, bankruptcies and so much more.

Strategies for hard times are important to have as part of your marketing arsenal. Difficult times require us to work harder, to focus our energies on strategies and services that have the greatest potential for success. We need to be flexible and creative, seeking ways to help our clients. Even more than ever, our marketing strategies need to be highly focused on what will most benefit our potential and past clients - not only on what we hope to gain personally.

The Economic Climate

You should know there has been an economic recession every ten years since 1780 and there is no reason to believe that will change. As a matter of fact, we may now see the economic cycle swing from one extreme to another even more frequently, or we may see down cycles last longer than usual. There is no doubt that we are in a more uncertain decade than ever before in US history.

A wise business person will know where they are in relation to these cycles and be prepared with strategies for times of business slowdown. Depending on where you are located, these cycles may be more severe than other parts of the country. Regardless of that, we all tend to feel the fluctuations of the economy during an economic slowdown.

The decorating business, no matter what area of specialization, is considered part of the frills of life. When the economy is down, the frills are the first to be cut back or eliminated and the last to recover. You need to know that going in and be prepared for it. Fortunately, this aspect of home decor has millions of prospects, unlike other businesses whose target market is very small, plus it is much more affordable than full service interior design.

In a tough economy, find things that you can offer clients and prospects that are completely free or that will save them money. These *bonuses* might very well make the difference! Actually, people like bonuses no matter what the economy is doing. You can collect articles from magazines, the newspaper home and garden sections, reading books -- just about any where. You can give this information to your client for free. They will appreciate you, remember you favorably and, hopefully, pass your name and phone number on to someone else.

Merchant Account

This is one good reason to consider setting up a credit card merchant account. Don't do it until you have started to get some regular business, but you are going to find prospects that will balk at paying your services by cash or check but who would still be willing to schedule a consultation if they can pay by credit card.

I have my merchant provider services set up on my web site so that people can purchase my eBooks and reports and other accessories with a credit card. It is therefore no problem to offer credit when I am setting up appointments. All you need to have is a form to fill out the particulars of the price and gather the credit card number, expiration date and a signature from your client when you arrive on the appointment. Later you can process it manually over the internet.

Continuing Education

Never stop learning. It's really important for you to continue to grow, both professionally and personally. Look for seminars, classes you can take, books you can read -- grow your mind and your creativity.

This is how I have been able to develop so many exclusive products. I like exclusivity. It means you're the only one who has it. Exclusive products promote your expertise.

Age doesn't matter. Go back to college. Get away from the TV and dive into a good marketing book. Get up earlier and take that seminar. I always feel that if I can come away from any kind of self-education effort with *one good idea*, then it has been worthwhile.

But don't just be a collector of good ideas. If you don't put them to work for you, they are valueless. So when you get a good idea, no matter what it's source, put it into practice immediately. The more time that goes by from the idea being planted in your mind, the less likely you are to ever use it. So act upon your newly gained knowledge immediately.

The Savings Rule

I hope you agree with me that all of our blessings come from God. I appreciate what He has given to me. I recognize that all wealth and power belong to Him and He wants me to devote a small percentage of what He has given to me back to Him. As a Christian, I faithfully give a percentage of what I earn to help other people. I know that He has promised to meet my every need and He has. When you give to help others, and do so as abundantly as you can, it will come back to you many times over.

I also recommend that you practice the very strategic and economically sound policy of putting aside 10% of your earnings into a savings plan or some other kind of investment portfolio and let this money start to *work for you*. Don't be someone who is always working for money - create ways for money to work for you. Look in your local Yellow Pages for a professional financial consultant. They will be happy to discuss the issue with you and help you plan for the future.

Always pay yourself. Put some money aside for investments, particularly passive income investments. Put aside some for continuing education because you must never stop learning. Put away some to play and some for long term purchases and some for emergencies. Create a habit of doing this every month and your wealth will grow.

The Strategy of Preeminence

I've saved this for last because it is the core belief system that drives everything I do, stand for, teach, and create. It's the foundation that my consulting, publishing and design business is built upon. It's the one key fundamental I teach above and beyond anything else in every consultation I perform and in every product or service I offer.

I saved it for last so that it will be the last concept you read and hopefully the one you treasure. **This is the single most important segment of this Primer.**

"I have a very simple philosophy on life. You shouldn't steal from yourself. If you're going to commit your life to an enterprise, wealth creation, the security and the financial well-being of your family . . . and if other people -- your staff, your team, your employees, your vendors -- are going to commit their lives to you, you owe it to yourself and to everyone else to get the highest and best results. You should never accept a fraction of the yield when with the same effort or less, the same people or fewer, the same time or less, the same capital or less, the same opportunity cost or less, can deliver so much more to you currently and perpetually."
-- Jay Abraham (multi-million dollar marketing guru)

This quote is from the president of one of the most successful entities of its kind in the United States. His business is approximately 400% larger than his closest competitor. His company has grown 15 times in the last five years. It is ten times more profitable. It commands an absolute, unequivocal predominance in every area that it has penetrated. His people have more fun, they are more formidable and they are more invincible than anyone I have ever me, and probably than anyone you have ever met.

This is the foundational pillar of their success.

They strove to have enormous empathy with their clients.

They saw their purpose as leadership. They saw their purpose and their role as being a leader, an authoritative, consultative force in their marketplace. They believed it was essential that they telegraph and communicate and convey to their prospects and clients that they shared common feelings. In other words, "I feel the way you feel. I understand what your problem is."

They understood there was a distinct difference between giving information and giving advice. They worked hard at letting people know that their role was, "Here's what you should do about a problem, situation or opportunity." Then after that, they supported their solution with a compelling, irrefutable definitive set of facts. They saw their role as helping people focus on issues they had never verbalized.

Their view, which should be yours, was to present views their clients could trust. They saw their role, their function, their purpose, their advantage, their positioning as being a leadership authority -- but also they saw their role as being benevolent, nurturing and loving.

Be the refreshing, distinctive alternative to the mundane and the unfulfilling norm. Don't strive to be main stream because people think that mainstream is a commodity. Mainstream is not distinctive. Mainstream has little value. No one wants to feel like a commodity. Commodities have no purpose. They have no connectivity.

Show them the truth as you see it. Help them take the next step. Connect the dots for them, give them a plan, help them take the next step, protect them from making errors, make the steps logical, appropriate, obvious and easy. Listen to them, see what they want even if they can't, and then help them achieve what they can't even put into words.

Try not to be self serving in your efforts to be selfless. It will show. Take your belief system and direct it outwards -- towards the benefit of others. If you can genuinely see your higher cause or purpose on this earth as being to enrich other people's lives, to bring them greater benefits, greater protection, greater advantage, greater financial benefit, greater savings, greater safety, greater productivity -- greater whatever it is -- then you will surely achieve total fulfillment and success cannot help but come your way in time.

So if you want your business to really soar, have a passionate awareness and commitment to a higher purpose beyond your own self enrichment. Focus on helping other people's lives be better, help other people become more fulfilled, help other people get more out of the process and out of life and home.

Embrace every client's situation with hope and promise. This is my wish for you too -- that you will get so much more out of everything you do. I hope you will allow yourself to get so much more productivity, profitability, connectivity and residual value out of every action, every hour, every dialogue, every contact, every client.

If you can communicate those sentiments to your prospects and clients, and if you look at everyone you meet or talk to in that way, you will gain a new and deeper appreciation of them. You will have a lot more respect for them. And you will generate those same feelings out of them toward you.

Remember these simple questions and ask them of yourself often:

1) What problems am I going to help my clients solve?

2) How can I have the most positive impact on the people I'm trying to reach?

3) If I were on the receiving end, why would I want this service?

4) If I were on the receiving end, what's in it for me?

Learn to love your clients. It's the most valuable gift you will ever give them.

In conclusion, I encourage you to constantly seek ways to enrich, protect and enhance as many lives as you can. If you do that, I can guarantee you that you will create value, livelihood and fulfillment for yourself and your life will become quite profound. Take full advantage of your true purpose.

I submit to you that until and unless you understand that you have a higher purpose for being in this business or any business, you can't begin to take advantage of your full potential. Your purpose cannot and should not be to get rich or you will never get there. Your purpose must be to see what you can do for others and what you've already done for them.

Most people fall in love with their product or their company. Instead, fall in love with your client. If you can't, you're in the wrong business or you don't appreciate your business or you don't appreciate your worth.

Most people think, "What do I have to say to get people to hire me?" Instead say to yourself, "What do I have to give? What benefit do I have to render?" Actually the Bible said it already thousands of years ago: "Do unto others as you would have them do unto you."

Become a value creator. The more value you give others, the more value you generate (not for yourself but for your clients). The more contribution you make to the richness of their lives, the more successful you will become and the more bonded you will be to them -- and they to you.

Homeowners need solutions, not strategy. Now go show them what you have to give.

Chapter Twelve

A Potpourri of Cool and Effective Marketing Ideas

Letter Submitted by Jacqueline E Ball, IDC, Wichita, KS

Hello, Barbara, I noticed your marketing contest on your site and thought it was great idea. I wanted to share one I have always used with you that has been very beneficial for me. Years ago, I came up with a marketing concept that created instant clientele and future prospects for my services. I spun the idea from typical home parties and decided to create what I called in-home re-arranging seminars. The hostess volunteers to furnish one room and a dozen fee paying attendants. Targeted prospects are the homeowners family, friends, co-workers, or even neighbors all sharing an interest in learning how to refurbish their own homes in a cozy and familiar environment. Each person would receive a little informational packet regarding basic re-arranging info, concepts and tips and hands-on training....for an attendance fee.

The hostess benefits by having a room rearranged for free. I benefit because she supplies the home, furnishings and paying students. Each one of those people knows other people....and the word of mouth theory carried on and created quite a buzz for my business. As you know, you can show people how to rearrange things....but many times, when left to their own devices....they still have no clue or little creativity to put what they learned from the demonstration to use in their actual home settings, which can be to my advantage as well. The in-home parties are a win-win situation for everyone and a great marketing tool. I was curious to know if you have ever tried this idea in your area and if you had how it worked for you.

Marketing Interview with Jacqueline by Barbara Jennings

Barbara: - J.E., that is a really terrific concept and I thank you for sharing it with me. I will pass it on to others and give you the credit for the idea. No, I never did anything like that, though I once did the party plan concept for Tupperware (in my youth) and for an art company (about 20 years ago). I didn't care for the setting, because I have to admit I was shy of asking for referrals in those days, so it proved to be not as effective for me personally, though other people found it to be quite easy.

Jacqueline: I know exactly how you must have felt, prior to becoming a certified personal coach....I could market anyone except myself...I was embarrassed to push or sell ....."me".

Barbara: - In your letter you mention, " . . You can show people how to rearrange things . . . but. . . when left to their own devices . . . still need help." I totally agree. You can give out all the concepts in the world, and people still have trouble making the application to their own situation. This is why I offer to respond personally to any questions my readers might have.

Jacqueline: Exactly....which was another reason, I chose to purchase your book, you offer an invaluable service to people far beyond what most authors of any book format do....I know, I research everything prior to purchasing...I want the best info available and I felt yours was far superior than others I had read. You go beyond and answer the "what-if questions" that others ignore.

Barbara: - I have a few questions I hope you'll answer.

Jacqueline: Absolutely...I always share whatever I have if it can be of some benefit to others.

Barbara: - Might I ask what the fee was that the "students" paid to attend and the average number of friends that paid to attend?

Jacqueline: When the idea was born, I was a young designer and only charged $25 per person. I quickly realized...depending on the "income level..." I could command more. I drew the time out.... which always makes people feel like they are getting their money's worth...I can kill an hour or two with Q/A sessions. As I became seasoned and gained a reputation with high end ladies.... I was commanding $75 per person....for one little afternoon. (3 to 4 hours).

Barbara: - Did the students pay you upon arrival or did they pay the hostess? How was that handled?

Jacqueline: This was trial and error...allow me to save you the trouble...when the students come in.... they 'register' and receive their Re-arranging Info Packet...which looks impressive to a novice. In order to register...they fill out their personal info and pay the fee and when that is completed they receive their packet....get that all out of the way from the get go....besides.....women love to get a package of things...it's like all their hopes are in a bag...:) By the way here's a tip... anytime you label it with Decorating Diva or Decorating Goddess kind of labels....in the title.. many women become giddy and ....I'm usually booked up for 3 other parties before I ever leave the seminar...many women react silly over words like diva and goddess....(but, hey...whatever makes them happy...it's all about marketing).

Barbara: - Did you have any minimum number of students the hostess had to provide?

Jacqueline: When I began, Barbara....I would go out for 3 or 5 and then.....I got older, wiser and set a minimum for 8 or 10. I never wanted to go over 12 because that's a lot of bodies to fit in some rooms. I wanted everyone to feel as if they had a chance to learn, ask questions and partake in the actual arranging...and get ready to sit back...because you are the director...everyone else does the actual "moving". They love it...however, be sure to have each one sign the waiver, during registration... better to play it safe.

Barbara: - Did any try to attend without paying?

Jacqueline: No, because they didn't get passed the register table....I only had trouble if I did the service first.

Barbara: - What happened if the attendees fell below the minimum?

Jacqueline: It all depends...how far I had to travel....(my mood...;)..who was hosting the party.... but the catch here, Barbara...is in the hosting ploy...When you advertise this service... write up something that sounds like this....ONE FREE ROOM RE-DECORATING for the hostess who provides....10 paying people....(a $500 value!)...if the hostess can only get 6 people...then she pays half of her fee....The goal for the hostess is to make the magic number of attendees and thereby having an entire room rearranged for free by a pro. Always put a dollar value on what they are receiving...you are dead-on about people not appreciating what they don't have to pay for.....!

Barbara: - Did you do the rearrangement right then in front of the people, or before or after the "seminar"?

Jacqueline: Always contact the person and see their home first.....prior to doing the party.... get digital photos of before....if at all possible....so you can have time to look the room over prior to designing on demand...so to speak. I leave the room as I find it....and when all are in place....I ask for volunteers.....to do the hands-on rearranging.....and then I direct. I naturally fall into an authoritative or leader roll....which, you sound as if you do as well... We direct... they follow and they actually feel they are being "trained". Nothing better than being taught by example....you know. Oh....here's another tip....I always take my accessories with me....I never have failed to sell out....at a party....they feel like they "have to have"....whatever "decorator's pillow" I have....etc.etc...

Barbara: - Since most people hire designers by word of mouth, or people they have already known or met, it's an excellent way of building rapport early on.

Jacqueline: Exactly....and people have witnessed...the process and go and tell their family, friends, neighbors...etc...It's free advertising and most of them keep their info packet and refer to it. The ones who are still basically clueless feel more comfortable and flat out hire me to do their homes...others refer me on and I get bookings...so it's a WIN/WIN EFFECTIVE TOOL....for all:) I also offer something extra to anyone who will go ahead and "book" another party that day. Say, 30% off any accessories or...half off the fee for a friend...that bring-a-friend thing really works well too.

oh and ....do offer "gift certificates"....to attend your parties...mother-in-laws love to give these to their daughter-in-laws...Okay...you get the idea...I know you probably are thinking..."info-over-load" ......but there's just a lot of little things that can really make a difference!

Barbara: - Terrific idea.

Jacqueline: Thanks:) I hope it serves you well...I know with your talents, skills and expertise you will be able to make this fly in a big way, Barbara...you are so far head of the game because you have already written your books...etc. I would suggest having your books with you....or as part of the fee...when people see you in action......they will WANT MORE!

Marketing Interview with Tracy Froment, Cumberland, RI

Barbara: Tracy, you're doing so well in your redesign business, I was wondering if you'd mind sharing some of your best tactics for marketing yourself and your services so my readers could benefit from your experience and success?

Tracy: I am doing ok in regards to getting business, I really believe it is due to the Lord blessing and having mercy on me:-). But here is my answer on what I've done so far. I live on a very busy state road which intersects with several affluent towns. I was able to place a sign advertising my business right on my property. Your clients will need to check how the zoning laws work in their town. My sign is only 18"x18" that is all my town allows. But since there is so much commuter traffic that passes by to reach the interstate they all see my sign.

Writing the decorating column has helped. I also have magnetic car signs on my car doors. The price was $80 for two signs. So when I am out in the community people see the sign and I always keep business cards in my glove compartment. My website is visited on a regular basis due to my decorating column.

I have also gone to department stores and spoke to the store managers to see if I could set up a booth and answer decorating questions for customers. I am in the process of having an "Ask the Decorator Day" at a local curtain factory outlet. I am not getting paid, but it is free advertising for me and a good way to pass out business cards. I also had gift certificates made and I send them to the successful realtors in town. For example, I send out a letter with the first two gifts at no charge just enough to get them interested. Then I sell a $50 gift certificate for $25, and a $75 certificate sells for $35. They pass it on to their client as a thank you gift and when the client calls me to redeem it I end up with a consult and completing a written design plan. My profit is $250 instead of the usual $275.

Your readers can also do a free decorating seminar at their local library or YMCA. Just make sure the handouts reflect the topic they are discussing and staple a business card to it. My last tip is to take the weekly real-estate section from their local paper and send out a letter to the new home owners offering a 10-15% discount on services. I would first have someone design a logo for their business and then a complete stationary setup. I did a consult for a graphic artist, we worked out a plan that I would decorate her living room if she would create my logo and stationary. I paid $427 for the printing. If we had not worked out this deal, it would have cost me over $2000. She does packaging designs for many large companies, including design packaging for Harry & David products, so she is excellent.

See, I told you it's not me, it is the Lord. I have not paid to advertise in any paper. He just blesses. I am very grateful to have a heavenly father who has given me talent and now has opened the door for me to use it.

Barbara: I know you have a website too, Tracy. Can you tell me how it is working for you?

Tracy: Here it goes :-) a lot of my calls come from my web site. If folks are serious about decorating, a web site is really an asset in today's market. They can call the college in their area and see if a student who will be graduating in year or so will do it for free or for half price. Most web designers are happy to do it free as they also need to create a portfolio. Research, research, research.

Barbara: How many visitors to your website do you get and how do you convert them into clients?

Tracy: I get about 5-7 hits a week, it doesn't sound like much. But my web guy, God bless him, I have no idea what he does, but I pray for him. He then sends me their e-mail address. I then e-mail them back thanking them for visiting my web site and offer 15% off my services. They call me most of the time or e-mail me back.

Barbara: Tracy, let me ask a few specific questions about what you said earlier. What wording did you put on your outdoor sign? This will not be an idea available to most people, but there might be a few who could do this type of thing.

Tracy: My sign is only 18"x18" so I could not get fancy. First line on the sign is very large print it says: Interiors; second line in small letters my business name, Interiors by Tracy Lee, third line in medium print Decorating Consultant, 4th line my phone number, same size print as first line, last line in medium print my web address. Most of my business comes from that sign.

Barbara: What wording did you put on the magnetic signs you have on your car?

Tracy: Car signs match my street sign. It takes a while for people to catch on. When I'm out, folks approach me and say, "Do you have a decorating business on a Diamond Hill Road?" Perfect opportunity to hand them business cards. Keep the car magnets and the street sign in the same color, same logo, same wording. The sign was made to fit my car doors. I paid $40 a piece for them. Well worth it.

Barbara: I haven't used the magnetic signs, but I do have custom license plate holders, mentioning my business as shown in the picture. How did you get the decorating column, for whom do you write, and how often?

Tracy: I e-mailed the editor of my local paper. I briefly introduced myself and told him about my business. I then asked if they would be interested in me writing a bi-weekly decorating column. I included ideas of what I would write about. I then asked could I do it in a question and answer format. They e-mailed me back requesting a meeting. Go to the meeting prepared, make extra copies of the topics you want to write about so if others are involved in the meeting you can have copies for everyone. At that same meeting, I pitched the idea of a decorating contest. I gave them some ideas and they were sold. My column is called "Decorating Made Simple & Easy". My picture runs with the column and it is free advertising! They post my business name and web address at the end of every column. Dress in business attire and be professional. For the contest, they are taking the before and after pictures of the contest and there advertisers are donating the furniture, carpet and window treatments. I'll do the design work, shop for the furnishings and accessories, and manage the project . It is free publicity. They also asked me to donate three $50 gift certificates, for the 3 runners up. I sure will, all that free advertising:-) A two page spread in the April home section. YOU BET!

Barbara: Can you briefly explain what's involved in setting up your booth for the "Ask a Decorator a Question" day?

Tracy: Let me use Target as an example, Middle America shops there. Call the store and ask if the store manager is in. If they you tell yes, thank them and make an excuse and get off the phone. Get dressed(professionally), take your packet of information and go to the store and meet with the manager. Explain what you want to do. The factory outlets love this stuff. If they agree, the morning of the event I walk around the store and gather accessories to create a pleasing colorful vignette using the stores merchandise. If your decorators have trouble accessing a store, approach a high quality consignment shop. Select a 2 hour window and have fun with it.

What you need for decorators day is packets. I have typed up handouts on the following ideas: creating a color scheme, where to get inspiration from, creating vignettes, how to mix pattern. I then take a color photo of a room in my house after I stage it. I copy it in color, blow it up and that is the cover page for the handouts. I purchased clear plastic folders from Staples Office Supply Store and I put it in a nice package for the consumer. Again they feel they are getting something of value. Always include your business card.

Barbara: What do you say in your letter to the realtors?

Tracy: I introduce myself, telling them about my business. (I do not use the letter anymore as my business is growing faster than I can handle it.) I then ask them if they want to give their clients a unique gift. How about the gift of decorating? Your clients will be so grateful. I then include two $50 complimentary gift certificates. I include a future price list, $50 certificates can be purchased for $25, $75 at $35, $100 at $50. They like it because they are getting a deal and I also win because I get the consult. Be brief they do not want to read a lot of information, they are busy, so keep it short and to the point.

Barbara: What do you say in your letter to the new homeowners?

Tracy: I am attaching the letter, feel free to tweak it or use it. I also had a two-sided post card made up. One side is my business logo and information. The other side is all the services I provide, there is also a 15% discount off my services. I leave it at the better shops, Antique shops, High quality consignments shops etc. and privately owned furniture stores.

Dear Mr. and Mrs. XXXXXXX;

Please allow me to introduce myself. My name is (insert your name here) and I am a Decorating Consultant. My home office is located at (insert your address here). Since you have recently purchased a new home you may find that you will need advice from an experienced decorator.

When purchasing a new home it can be difficult to make your existing furniture and accessories fit into the new space. Please don't make the mistake of purchasing new items and spending your money unnecessarily. As a new home owner, **allow me to save you money by giving you a 25% discount on my usual consultation fee.**

Please consider:

1.   Decorators have many cost effective ways to decorate your home.
2.   Decorators can save you money, because we can help avoid making unnecessary purchases. We can advise you on what is needed, saving you time and money.
3.   Decorators can look at your existing accessories and furniture and help rearrange your rooms without you spending a dime.
4.   With time being such a valuable commodity these days, we can make suggestions and/or do all the leg work (i.e. purchasing Paint, wallpaper etc.) leaving you time to be with your family.

Please call me at (xxx) xxx-xxxx or e-mail me at xxx@xxxx if you have any questions regarding your decorating needs.

Getting People to Call You!

Wouldn't it be nice if people just picked up the phone and called you and begged you to come do a redesign for them? I've had it happen, but the norm for most re-designers is that they have to pursue leads and referrals. This is especially true when you are just starting your business. That's the name of the game - no matter what business you are in.

But let's take another approach at least for discussion sake and see if you find a fit for yourself . . .

Step 1. You've got to interrupt their thoughts

As a society we are so inundated with information overload that it is very easy to tune out important messages we might wish we were receiving. I'm ashamed to admit that there are times I'll be working and a co-worker, friend or family member will speak to me as they are leaving. I am so absorbed in what I am doing, I don't even "hear" them, much less acknowledge them. I've learned how to tune out background noises and fully focus on what I'm doing. Other people are the same way. So you've got to reach out and GRAB their attention.

You can do this by...

- Having bold, compelling headlines
- Unusual graphics or photos
- Unique opening statements

One savvy marketer runs ads in a pricey magazine. He grabs attention simply by running his ad up-side-down. This one little trick makes this 2x2 inch ad pull as well for him as a 1/4 page ad, which would cost immensely more.

Look for ways to grab someone's attention. Years ago I wasn't getting anywhere sending out my press releases for *Where There's a Wall – There's a Way*. Then I changed my slogan to, "101 Ways to Dress a Naked Wall". Wow! What a difference. I even used that little headline in my online pay-per-click advertising, but I changed it when I discovered I was getting all of the WRONG kind of visitors who were titillated by the word 'naked' in the subheading. So you do have to be careful. But the point is still valid. When you grab someone's attention, you have a chance to get your message thru.

Step 2. Make your content relevant to them

Relevant content is so important once you have their attention. I'm sure we have all been tricked by email spammers into opening an email because the subject category was intriguing, only to find that it was someone selling something which had nothing to do with the headline. The content needs to be relevant to the headline and it needs to include helpful information which is relevant and of interest to your prospect. I have no interest in how to repair cars, so a headline that says, "How to Repair Your Car in 30 Minutes" will be of no value to me, no matter how good the training is.

It's not relevant to me.

But if I saw a headline that said, "How to Buy Furniture for Your Home at 75% Off Retail", I would probably take the bait. And so would you, you know you would. So you see your message must be relevant and of interest to your prospect.

Step 3. Solve a problem through education

Education-Based Marketing is one of the most powerful marketing strategies available today. When you have grabbed their attention and the message is relevant to them, then is the perfect time to educate them and this will do a number of good things for you:

- It gives your prospect the REASON WHY they should care about what you're saying.
- It appeals to the prospect's emotional need to solve their problem. (People buy with their emotions - especially women)
- It positions you as the expert and someone to be trusted.

For instance, why do you think you find all those long, long sales letters on the internet? Mine are very, very long. The reason I use them is because they work! The more you tell the more you sell. To be honest, this is one reason I create a newsletter every month. While I really want to help you become successful, I also want to be more successful myself. So I use education-based marketing concepts all the time.

Step 4. Then prove your solution really works

People today are so SKEPTICAL. We've all been duped at one time or another. It's not a good feeling and none of us like it. We've, therefore, come to be very wary of anyone pitching a message to us, no matter how genuinely good their product or service might be. No one believes anybody anymore. Every marketing message is taken with a grain of salt.

That's why it's vitally important to prove what you're saying is true. You can prove your truthfulness in a variety of ways: customer testimonials, findings from studies or surveys, quotes from experts, your before and after photos. This is another reason why I have made some of my "before and after" photos available to you to use. My CD slideshow is my way of **loaning** you the proof you need until you get some of your own. So if you haven't ordered a set of at least 6 of the CDs, you are really failing to give your business the essential marketing tools you need to help you really DO this business. The CD slideshow is the perfect tool to prove your case

Think of yourself sitting in a court room, on trial to prove your case. Think of your prospects as the jury, listening with a wary eye to see if any part of your testimony is false.

Are you proving your solution in your marketing efforts? If you are not, you will most likely fail. People buy what they want and need, but they ONLY buy from people they feel they can trust. Showing PROOF of what you do, with before and after pictures, will ensure them that you are a trustworthy person.

Step 5. Offer them additional help for their problem

Now that you have teased them and peaked their interest, you must close the deal by calling them to some kind of action: here is where you would offer them something like a free report, a video, one of my CD slideshow presentations, free answers to questions and so forth.

However, bear this in mind. You want REAL prospects, people who are seriously interested. It does you little good to be sending out free reports, CDs or anything else to some people. So to make sure your prospects are really legitimate, you may want to decrease your response and increase the quality of prospects that come to you. In that event you can charge a small fee to make the next step.

Step 6. Make sure you know what you're doing

If you do not have a degree in interior design, then you really MUST get the proper design training. I don't mean a degree – but proper rearrangement training for furniture and accessories. You will face a client now and then who quizzes you on why you are doing what you are doing, wanting to know the design concept behind your decisions. You may have a knack for knowing how to arrange things, but if you cannot back up your decisions with solid concepts, you will look and sound unprofessional. There is nothing worse than being in a client's home and presenting yourself as a professional and then being unable to solve their problems. Also bad is being asked questions by a client and not knowing how to answer the question with an authoritative answer. So it is imperative that you know what you are doing so that your clients will not only love the end result, but greatly appreciate your educating them regarding the design concepts you employed.

Generating Plenty of Referrals!

Referrals are the lifeblood of any small business and most certainly they are very important to a re-designer or an art consultant. In fact, surveys show that the vast majority of all new customers, clients, and patients come from referrals. Why are referrals so powerful? Well, because the person that has been referred to you already has a degree of trust in you, simply because you were referred by someone they know. And trust is everything. No one will hire you to do anything if they do not trust you and like you. Successful re-designers and art consultant's are likable people, as well as trustworthy people.

We all know that we should be getting more referrals so why then is it that the very best referral generating companies only produce a fraction of what they could be getting? Let's see why.

Why Most Businesses Aren't Getting All the Referrals They Could and Should be Getting

You see, most small businesses get their referrals from customers. That's okay, but the truth is...the majority of referrals should be coming from businesses that provide complimentary products and services.

90% of your referrals should be coming from complimentary businesses, NOT your customers. This is such an important and vital concept, the savvy internet businesses use it all of the time, not only to get referral traffic, but to get better rankings from the search engines. It's called reciprocal linking.

It's much more difficult to set up a systemic referral program that brings in predictable and consistent results from customers. Word of mouth from my trainees and visitors is great when it happens, but it is difficult to get. Thankfully there have been many, many trainees who have written me unsolicited testimonials, but for every testimonial I have received, the vast majority of my clients never refer me on to their family, friends or co-workers. They just don't think to do it.

However, businesses that sell complimentary products and services can easily be motivated to consistently send you referrals....if you set up your referral systems correctly.

In reality, there's no end to the different types of joint venture referral relationships you can establish with complimentary businesses. Both you and those businesses are reaching the same target market with non-competing products and services.

Do This Short Exercise to See What I Mean...

Step 1

Take out a clean sheet of paper and draw a line down the middle of the paper.

Step 2

Now list all the "types" of businesses that provide complimentary products and services on the left side of the paper leaving spaces in between.

For instance, for a re-designer, some complimentary businesses might be...

1. a house painter, 2. a real estate agent 3. a landscaper....

Step 3

Then on the right side of the paper, make a list of all the local businesses in your area that fall under each type of category.

For instance, you might have five different painters in the area or 50 different real estate agents. List them all.

Step 4

Now take some time to think about what you could offer them in return for them to send you a referral. Use your imagination.

If you really think about it you'll be able to come up with some great ideas.

Step 5

Lastly, it's time to go out and propose your referral systems ideas to your potential joint venture partners.

What you'll find is that some just won't *get it*. They won't have the vision it takes to accept your proposal.

But you'll also find a lot of business owners that are hungry to grow their business and are happy to discuss the possibilities. You may even find they will be looking to get referrals from you in return. That way you don't need to spend any money or exchange anything other than information.

Those are the type of people that can potentially bring you large quantities of highly qualified referrals.

So what's stopping you?

Success doesn't just happen. You've got to make it happen. Sharpen your designing, decorating skills. Yes. Be trustworthy. Be likeable. All of that is very, very important.

But you've got to get your products or service in front of people. They have to hear about you. They have to be presented with great reasons why they will benefit from your product or service.

If you fail to get the word out, you will fail and it won't matter how nice you are, how trustworthy you are or how much talent you have.

It's a numbers game. For every "no" you get, you will be just that much closer to your next "yes".

And since we are in a very visual business, don't rely solely on your ability to verbalize what you do. 95% of people are **visual learners**. That means they have to **see** what you do, not just **hear** about it.

So if you haven't yet ordered your set of the CD Slideshows which will dramatically help you **show** people just what you can do, and give them fantastic reasons why they need you, then you are losing out on money that could be falling into your pocket - guaranteed.

5 Ways to Reach Your Niche Market and Convert Them

I've been asked to share some marketing mediums which have worked for consultants of all types of businesses when trying to reach their small niche market. This is one of the most common questions re-designers and consultants ask. Here are 5 Mediums You Could Successfully Use to Reach Your Niche Market...

1. Niche Related Websites

Create a website for your business, whether you do it yourself or you hire someone to do it for you. Nowadays people are using the internet more and more to search for what they want. In addition to that, just having some pages of free content on your website will give you the kind of credibility you need to allay any apprehensions a prospect might have regarding your abilities.

2. Trade Magazines

Small classified ads in trade magazines can pay off nicely. You could place a small (2" x 2") ad. The downside is that you usually have to wait for 2 months before the publication will display your ad.

The key to advertising successfully is to try to reach really targeted traffic, not general traffic. So never pick a magazine that is not primarily focused on decorating.

3. Pay-Per-Click Search Engines

PPC's are a way many people are generating traffic to their website. The results from paid "ads" are not as good as those from the free listings, but they can still pay off for you if you write good copy and make it as easy as possible to hire you..

4. Rented Lists

You can rent a targeted address for around $.05 - $.08. The secret to using rented lists is to NOT sell them anything, but to get them to respond to a free report or an inexpensive gift that you can send to them with the real sales letter.

The whole goal is to capture their mailing address so you can write to them over and over again.

5. Targeted Trade Shows and Conventions

You've got to have some established credibility before you go after this method. Event planners really want to know you'll be able to deliver the goods you promise and that you are not over-reaching.

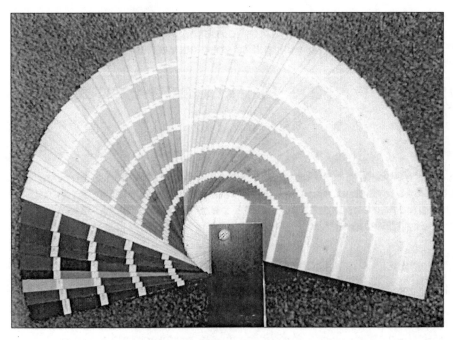

Do you know what a fan deck is? Do you know what the two Color Keys are and why knowing them is essential to giving good color consultations? If you can't answer these questions with a "yes", you need to take the design training for sure.

Chapter Thirteen

The Power of One

One of my all time favorite movies is called "The Power of One". If you haven't seen it, be sure to rent it from your local video store. It's an amazing story that takes place in South Africa during World War II. A waterfall is made up of billions and billions of tiny droplets. A single drop of water has very little power of its own. But put that drop with billions of other droplets - now you have power.

So what does this have to do with a redesign business or becoming a home stager? It's all about numbers, my friend. You may be only a single "drop of water", but when you connect with a vast number of other "droplets" all moving in the same direction at the same speed and at the same time, then all of you have become a "might force". And that's what you call a "waterfall".

I'm not talking about putting ads in the newspaper or a target magazine here like I was above. Nope. I'm talking about the power of publicity.

I'm right now on the verge of rolling out a huge publicity campaign for my own business. After investing in over $1000 worth of software, media lists and additional training, I plan to really blast news of my business in a dynamic way. So should you - at least eventually.

A Live Case Study

Here's a good example of what I'm talking about...

Many years ago a New Jersey man named Paul Hartunian began studying publicity and trying to figure out a system to help him get all of the publicity he could ever want for his various business ventures. One day he was watching TV news and saw that they were ripping up the wooden walkway of the Brooklyn Bridge. He saw the phone number of the construction company, called them up and inquired about what they were going to do with the wood. "Throw it away," was the response. He offered the man $500 to deliver all of the wood to him. Before the wood was even delivered, Hartunian had a press release all written and ready to release.

The headline of the press release said, "New Jersey Man Sells the Brooklyn Bridge for $14.95". He faxed a bunch of releases to media contacts he had acquired and literally within minutes his phone started ringing off the hook.

To make a long story short, Hartunian sold thousands and thousands of small pieces of wood, along with a certificate of authenticity, to people who called him by the droves to get one of the samples.

That initial press release then launched several successful decades of press releases all over the world on various products and services Mr. Hartunian sells and he has made a fortune.

You Can Do the Same Thing

It doesn't take a gimmick (like pieces from a famous landmark) to get news coverage. The best part about it is that it's always FREE and it will bring you far more potential clients than any kind of overt marketing, bar none.

Find out what is unique about you that would benefit someone else. The key is that whatever you write about must have a benefit to readers. Create a headline that grabs their attention. You only have a few seconds to get someone's attention. Make your article newsworthy by constantly asking yourself the question, "So what?"

Don't get bogged down in who you are or where you are or your background - none of that stuff - at least very, very minimal. Focus on the benefits the reader will derive. Benefits! Benefits! Benefits!

TESTIMONIAL
"My partner, Deborah, and I have been doing this for years and finally decided to get paid for it. We read your eBook and it has helped us launch a very successful redesign business. No one else in our area offers these services! It is really like getting paid to have fun! . . . With newspaper articles and speaking engagements, we have created a "buzz" in our area (previously untapped market) and are desperately trying to keep up with the calls. Thank you for all your help! - Lisette Dell'Apa"

Gearing Up for a Prosperous Business

Returning to the Basics

No matter what time of year it is now, you should begin your business with some well-thought-out goals. As I said earlier, if you don't know where you're headed, you're going to wind up somewhere else. You need short term goals and you need long term goals. So here are some extra tips to guide you along the way.

It's not enough to say to yourself, "Well, I just want to do better." That's not a goal; it's just wishful thinking. To be effective, goals must be specific. They must cause you to have to stretch to achieve them, but they must be realistic and achievable.

One of my goals in the beginning was to double my income from the previous year. I knew exactly how much I had made in the previous year, so the goal of doubling that income was very specific. I didn't know how realistic it was, but I knew that the only possible way anyone could double their income from one year to the next was by being an entrepreneur.

Well, I eventually increased my income by 80%, nearly achieving my goal! In prior years when I worked for someone else, I was never able to increase my income by 80% year over year.

When you consider the income potential we have as entrepreneurs, coupled with the freedom to be our own boss, work from home, set our own goals and hours, this is an amazing opportunity. But it all starts with having a plan for the year that is specific, detailed, easy to implement, easy to maintain. Because anyone who has ever been successful in any business will quickly tell you that it just doesn't *happen.* It takes work; it takes dedication; it takes focus.

You Must Have a Plan

Whenever I hear someone complain that their business isn't going well, my first thought is: "Well, what are you doing to promote your business? How many people have you talked to today?"

Years ago when I was first starting out as a corporate art consultant, a few years prior to adding re-design to my services, I began to do *cold calling.* This meant that I picked up the phone and made calls to strangers to drum up business. I was too inexperienced at the time to understand that cold calling is an extremely difficult way to promote a business. So I was easily discouraged.

When I commented on it to my partner, he asked me, "How many people did you talk to today?" I said, "Four." He burst out laughing. "Four??? You only talked to four people??? Barb, there are millions of people out there! You only talked to four??"

Ok, ok, stop laughing. I was a dope, I admit it.

The key to any successful adventure is the effective communication to others of what you have to offer that will benefit them. It's also a *numbers game.* Obviously the more people who hear or see what you have to offer, the greater chance of success you will have.

I've said it before. It bears repeating. People are only interested in what's in it for them. So if your message isn't getting out, and if it's not getting out in a manner that immediately tells them how they will benefit, all your hopes and dreams will go up in smoke instantly.

So what plan have you developed this year to market your business next year?

Essentials for a Basic Marketing Plan

- Put it in writing. Whatever you decide to do next year, put it in writing and put it up where you'll see it often as a reminder.
- Assign a dollar amount to what you want to make for the entire year. Break it down into how much you must earn each month on average to achieve your goal. Break that down further by dividing that amount by 4 so you know how much you need to average each week. Divide that by 5 so you know what your daily average should be.
- By knowing what your daily income average needs to be, what your weekly average needs to be, you will automatically have a constant mental reminder to help you gauge your efforts.
- Plan your daily, weekly, monthly schedule so that 80% of your time and effort is going into *promoting* your business, not *doing it.* I know, I know, I know. It's a lot more fun to DO it than to PROMOTE it. After all, doing it is creative. But you've got to recognize that the key to long term success is promotion.
- Put into play no less than 5 methods, that you do over and over again, to get referrals. Call people up. Write to them. Give them a little form to fill out. Don't ask for more than 2 names. Ask them to talk to the people first about you, then follow up with a phone call.

- Get 5 friends, co-workers, relatives to agree to invite people in for a mini redesign seminar. Charge each person attending a small fee. Do an actual redesign for the hostess, letting everyone participate. It can be very fun and profitable too. Then book appointments on the spot.
- Sit down and think of newsworthy aspects about you and your business. Write an article, always asking yourself the question, "Who cares?" When you have something written that will be very interesting or informative that people will care about, then you have a good press release. Send it out to all your local newspapers, TV stations, radio stations.
- Get your website launched if you haven't already.
- Have a license plate frame made that promotes your business. They cost around $12-20. Your vehicle can promote you wherever you go, but you've got to get advertising on it first. If you don't mind more blatant advertising, have a magnetic sign made that can be attached to the doors on each side of your car that is benefit driven.
- Hand out business cards, brochures where ever you go.
- Contact churches, women's groups and associations and offer to be a speaker. Donate a couple of free redesigns as prizes. Set up a nice vignette that is decorative. It doesn't have to be elaborate. Put together a chair, some coordinating fabric, a framed picture, a little table, a lamp, and some books. You hardly have to even mention your expertise: you've just shown them you know what you're doing.
- Get a set of the musical slideshow CDs. I now offer them in a set of 3, 6 or 12. You're not marketing effectively if you aren't using these to help you give people a pictorial idea of what a redesign service could do for them. The more you have circulating for you, the more you increase your chances of booking appointments. It's a numbers game. Never forget that.
- Get yourself a large calendar and hang it in your kitchen. Stare at the blank spaces until it bugs you to death. Then begin to write each day on the calendar what you will do that day to promote your business. As the spaces begin to fill up with activity, you will know you're focused correctly on promoting your business. At the end of each week, each month you'll be able to see how much targeted activity you actually did. This by itself will encourage you and keep you moving in the right direction.
- Every time you get an appointment, land a press release, get a speaking engagement, make a sale, write it on the calendar in large colored letters to separate it from the promotional activities.
- Every time you make money, take 10% for additional promotional efforts, 10% to save and spend 10% on yourself as a treat for a job well done.

Ok, did you notice that out of the list above, there's practically nothing on the list that doesn't involve the promotion of your business. And lest you think that you're being pushy, or too self-serving - think of this. You are doing your friends, family, co-workers, acquaintances a dis-service if you don't let them know what you can do for them. Everyone deserves to live comfortably. Everyone deserves to enjoy their home to the fullest. If they are selling their home, they deserve to get it sold in the shortest amount of time possible for the highest sales price. If you're an art consultant, everyone deserves to work in a space that is pleasing to the eye and pleasant to be in.

So if you're not sharing your talents and expertise with people, you are cheating them out of real tangible benefits that will improve their quality of life. And you'll be cheating yourself as well. So get up, get moving, start planning and then execute the plan. And may all your dreams and goals come true next year.

Getting and Staying Organized

Organizing really can be as easy as A-B-C, you just have to set your mind to it. It is also essential that you do this for the sake of your business, your family and your personal sanity. Here are 26 organizing ideas — one for each letter of the alphabet to help you get going, and, hopefully stay organized all year long.

Act Now While It's on Your Mind
Don't put it off until later. Later never seems to come. When you get an advertisement that interests you, if you lay it down to purchase later, you'll never do it, right? That is true for most of us in most things we do. So act upon something while it's in your hand or on your mind.

Break it Down Into Manageable Parts
Don't concentrate on the "whole", but break it apart into parts and focus on one part at a time. My 89 year old mother needed to pack for the hospital this week and just couldn't seem to focus on what to do until I reminded her it was real easy if she would set a date and time to complete and work on one small part of the process at a time. The way to move a mountain best is one shovel full at a time.

Containerize Your Business
I personally don't care for see thru containers but they work for some people. I prefer to "hide" my clutter, papers, and files. But I do take care to provide myself with a good desk, file drawers, shelves, boxes, baskets and so forth to place things into rather than having them strewn all around.

Delegate Some Chores to Others
Unless you work alone and live alone, you don't have to do everything all by yourself. Ask for help from family, friends, co-workers. You'd be amazed at how quickly a large task can be accomplished when everyone contributes just a little. You can always hire the services of an organizational specialist too. Make use of your computer, cell phone, answering machine, FAX and other equipment to streamline your procedures and processes. I have cut my support issues dramatically by putting detailed troubleshooting instructions on my website instead of answering each email on such subjects. So look for ways to cut down on time consuming details that could be handled more automatically.

Eliminate as Much Clutter as Possible
I can't think very well when my office gets overly messy as it does from time to time. So when that happens, I just stop everything I'm doing and de-clutter it. Take one day a week and devote to improving your work environment. You'll be amazed at how much better you function the rest of the week.

File It Away or Throw It Away
If you think you'll need it, file it in a logical place. If you aren't going to need it, throw it in the trash. Make the decision to do one or the other while the paper is in your hand. Don't let papers pile up on your desk until they become massive. The longer you wait, the less you will want to tackle the problem.

Give Things Away to Help Others
An old car I used to use for delivering art to clients sat in my driveway for years with the promise of my husband that he was going to fix it up and sell it. He never did. So a month ago I called a charity to come and get it. They will repair it and donate it to a needy family.

I get a tax write-off, but more importantly it feels good to have done something to help someone else in need.

Home is Where You Choose
Everything needs a "home" of it's own. I found myself wandering my office to find my glasses or my purse until I designated a special place to keep them. I religiously put them in that place and I have eliminated some wasted time and frustration from my life.

Identify Everything With Labels
As my eyesight has diminished, I needed a way to make large, readable and printed labels. While you can make labels on your computer, I chose to purchase a small, inexpensive label maker. It's so easy to identify everything in a box, a binder, a file folder when you can make quick, professional looking labels.

Judge Your Priorities
To successfully build any business, you need to spend most of your time "marketing" it, not "managing" it. So this requires you to prioritize what you're doing. I have set hours and days that I work. During my prime time hours, I only allow myself to do things that lead either directly or indirectly to making more money. All other chores are reserved for non prime time hours.

Knowledge Works
There are many ways to organize your business and life. Visit your local office supply store and just roam the aisles looking for products that will help you keep all of your business papers in order. Choose the system that takes the least amount of time and that makes sense for you.

Lists Help You Stay on Task
I am always far more organized and productive each day when I determine at least the day ahead what I will do that day. I rarely approach my day without a clear idea of what I want to accomplish that day. Sure there are surprises, but you need to plan and organize your daily tasks. A daily "to do" list really helps. Mine is broken into "calls to make", "things to buy", "emails to send", "things to take" and so forth.

Motivation Gets It Done
To me it always feels great to be able to cross things off my list that I have accomplished. It provides additional motivation to keep going. To motivate yourself, see yourself doing the task, finishing the task and rewarding yourself afterwards. Give yourself a time limit and see if you can beat it - kind of like playing a game with yourself.

"No" Can Be Very Powerful
None of us like to say "no" to anyone, usually, but you have to learn when to say "yes" and when to say "no". You can't imagine the destructiveness of long term stress, so you need to keep your goals and tasks manageable. Don't overload yourself or your schedule.

Order Out of Chaos
When you know where everything is, because it is all in it's proper place, you eliminate stress from your life. Seek to live an orderly life and run an orderly business. You will reduce your forgetfulness as well in the process because you'll be able to think better.

Planning and Preparation

Plan your month, your week and your daily activities. By planning what you want to accomplish, you'll be better able to prepare yourself properly. I hate to start a project, even cooking a meal, only to discover that I don't have a necessary ingredient or utensil to complete what I set out to do. Here is another way you can eliminate wasted time and energy by being prepared.

Quality Over Quantity

Choose your purchases with an eye for quality. You'll enjoy your possessions longer and in the long run, this makes them a better buy. Don't be a pack rat. If you haven't used something in a year, look for ways to dispose of it. Keep your life simple.

Reminders Keep You On Task

If I didn't have notes stuck around or a handy timer, I'd forget all kinds of things that are important to remember, just not important enough to lodge meaningfully on my brain. It gets worse the older you get, you know. I put notes on my desk, my computer, my door, my purse, my car, fridge - wherever I'll see them when I need to. Yeah, yeah, I know, it doesn't do anything for the decor, but remember, "Form follows function". Plus you can do as I do and get the post-its in decorator colors.

Sell - Sell - Sell

You don't make money if you don't sell your service or your product. That's why marketing is so important. Without strong marketing efforts, you can't sell. Be on the constant look out for better ways of presenting your service or product. Always be looking for more products to use as incentives, front end sales or back end sales.

Test Everything

Everything you own or do should pass a test. Testing is vitally important for all of your marketing strategies: test your advertising, test your sales pitch, test your prices, test your referral methods and so forth. If they don't pass the test, eliminate them.

Utilize All Your Space

Most of the time we only think about the usefulness of space within our grasp - that space that is eye level or below. But think vertically. How much space do you have from eye level to your ceiling? Could you more effectively make use of that space with cupboards, shelving or decoration? Look up and see how much more organizational space you really have.

Visualization and Conceptualization

The mind does not know the difference between what you emotionally visualize and what you actually do. You can literally teach yourself to type or play a piano through visualization, but only if you utilize all of your senses and emotions. If you regularly spend time visualizing yourself accomplishing great things in situations where you are apprehensive, you will ultimately be able to conquer those situations because your mind "believes" you have done so already.

Written Words Speak Louder

Any teacher worth her/his salt makes the student take notes. I make my electronic clients take notes by not letting them print out my eBooks. When you take notes your retention rises dramatically and you will retain what you learn far longer. Written words also convey an unspoken message of finality as they are believed to be non-negotiable. In business, make all of your agreements written to avoid misunderstandings and for the utmost legal protection.

X Means It Is Done

Use a large colored "X" to identify what you have accomplished on your "to do" list. Or if you cross an item off, do it in large colored ink, like with a marker. The feeling of self-satisfaction intensifies the larger it is. Then go celebrate your achievements.

Your Self Worth

Remember to take time for you. Everyone needs rest and relaxation, food, companionship, fun, shopping, creativity, spiritual input. Be sure to allocate time each day for your own rejuvenation.

Zone In - Not Out

Stay on task. Stay devoted to your dream. Stay enthusiastic. Be tenacious. In the end, it will pay off for you.

I can tolerate a small amount of mess, but if it gets pretty bad, I shut down mentally. I become useless. When my eyes started to lose focus and I had to resort to wearing reading glasses, it felt like I was spending half my day hunting for my glasses. This was frustrating and a complete waste of my valuable time and energy.

Being the organized soul that I am, it didn't take me long to figure out that I needed several pairs, not just one. So I purchased a pair for each desk, a pair for my purse and a pair for my keyboard (I don't play much, but it warranted an old pair).

All I have to remember now is to leave the assigned glasses at their assigned "stations".

Who Are the Influencers In Your Market?

- Marketing to "influencers" is simply smart marketing.
- It increases your return on marketing dollar because the Lifetime Value of an influencer is much higher due to the fact that they can bring you a lot of referrals.
- Who are the influencers in your market?
- Are you giving them special attention?
- Do you have a special marketing program just for them?
- Take some time to create a comprehensive list of the influencers in your market, then develop a special relationship marketing program tailored just for them.
- You'll find that your sales will go up and your marketing costs will go down...and who wouldn't want that?

Getting Complimentary Publicity

I've said before that it's really important to get your business known in your community. Complimentary publicity is one of the best ways to do that. The difference between publicity and advertising is not just in the price tag: one is complimentary, the other one isn't. But publicity acts like a third party recommendation, and readers are known to respond far better to publicity than to advertisements.

We're going to discuss some methods of getting publicity that you don't have to pay for with some more unusual tactics.

Throw some of these ideas into your marketing procedures and see what happens.

If you were a reporter and every day you had to hunt for a story or article, don't you think you'd like a little help from time to time? Where does a reporter go to find a story? Where do they find people?

Send a brief notice to your local TV or radio station and tell them that you specialize in a certain topic and that if they are ever in a hard spot to find someone to interview on that topic after they have called around, to give you a call. Ask them to put you in their rolodex. Most media people have a rolodex of local experts. You can telephone them or send them a letter.

Just call the reporter up and tell him/her you are an expert in this area and you would welcome any questions the reporter might have for you.

Publicity Referral Services

Would you like to be on the lists of experts that media people reference every day from all over the country? These lists are called "Publicity Referral Services". One such referral service is the RTIR Magazine, otherwise known as Radio-TV Interview Report.

You can find the online version at http://www.RTIR.com. These are all people who can be contacted for interviews for all kinds of media on the topic of their expertise. By becoming a member (there is a fee), you can start getting media calls requesting interviews. It's easy and it works. Some of the NY Times bestselling authors use this service.

Publicity Introduction Meetings

There are even meetings that you can pay to attend that will introduce you to media producers and editors at the highest levels? RTIR sponsors these types of events too. Think of it as a publicity networking meeting.

These top media people, producers and directors, are there to meet new people and hear your story. While they are pretty expensive to attend, whole careers and businesses have been launched by just one good contact.

As I am writing this, a National Publicity Summit is being conducted in New York City on July 14-17. For more information, visit www.NationalPublicitySummit.com.

Chapter Fourteen

Becoming a Leading Strategic Force

**Do you want faster growth and more profits
for your new business?**

Huge success doesn't come overnight - not for any business, and certainly not for a redesign, rearrangement business. The best opportunity you have to ignite explosive growth and stimulate profits is to invest your time, effort and capital to turn your business into a leading marketing force in the industry.

Winning companies dominate their competitors in two specific, primary ways: better business strategy and brilliant strategic marketing. All you have to sell, really, is your talent and your knowledge. That is all that separates you from your competitor, unless you have a design store or products you are selling specifically.

The best way to advance your company to the forefront, then, is through a world-class strategic marketing process that has been tested and refined by the "war rooms" of the most successful marketers on the planet today. Happily this business doesn't have a whole lot of competition, but you're still going to have to market your business smartly, wisely and continuously.

**Developing a Super Strategy -
The Secret to Winning in Today's Market**

Most businesses use a "tactical" marketing game which generally isn't all that successful, if at all. If you do the same thing, your results will be as poor as theirs. But if, instead, you reformulate, execute and fully deploy some "super strategies", it can distinctively and preemptively change the rules of the competitive game in redesign and give you a very distinct advantage.

A super strategy is the secret to winning wars and it's also the same secret to winning marketing wars. In a war, it's the difference between a stunning victory or a massive defeat. In marketing, it's the difference between failure or mediocrity and phenomenal success.

So to start you out correctly, I'll be pushing you to create a super strategy and focusing your total attention of building your business in that manner. Once you have created this custom strategy to meet your personal goals, you'll be able to marshal all the different marketing concepts into one unified, powerful, focused business building force that makes everything your business does from now on work 100 times better than before!

You'll be able to realistically target markets, customer segments, and positioning advantages that you want your business to dominate. This will allow you to literally "own" your market in your area and have the strategic mechanism to fully achieve each goal you set.

A marketing Super Strategy represents the most powerful form of growth hormones you can give to your business today. Nothing else you can do will produce the massive multiplier effect that strategic marketing, as opposed to tactical marketing, will deliver.

WHAT IS THE DIFFERENCE?

A Marketing Super Strategy is the "complete battle plan" -- the fully integrated master-vision and execution plan for your marketing that you formulate and perfect to accomplish the goals for your business. It must be sustainable and continuous. If you were building a home, it would be your blueprint. It's your layout of how everything in your business will fit together like a glove. It's the overall plan and the sum of all the parts of your business, all being headed in one single direction. And it's the only real way you will ever successfully produce the exponential results you are (or at least should be) after for your redesign business.

The Difference Between Tactics and Strategy

Strategy is the general plan for waging the war itself. Tactics are the multitude of specific tasks which achieve the strategic objective of the general plan. There is a big difference between super strategy and tactical marketing, one that most entrepreneurial marketers totally fail to realize, let alone seize upon.

I want to examine six critical, strategic ideas that can produce faster growth and higher profits for your business. My purpose is to get you to absolutely realize that investing more time and effort and capital on strategic marketing has tremendous potential to ignite explosive growth for you and give you competitive superiority over other designers and re-designers. Here they are:

1. Marketing strategically vs. marketing in a purely tactical way (the way 99% of all business operates) produces a MONSTER difference in results (up to 100 times greater results by marketing strategically)
2. Why you MUST use strategic marketing to put your business on a growth course for future profits, because without it you are destined to be mediocre, disappointed and out of business
3. How to effectively and optimally use strategic marketing in your business
4. How to overcome the key obstacles and crash the barriers to unleash the full potential of this kind of thinking
5. How to best utilize a Super Strategy
6. How to get a strategy mindset to rise above all of your competition altogether.

YOUR ULTIMATE GOAL

The ultimate goal you've got to pursue is to evolve your design business to thrive in your marketplace. You've got to produce products and service your customer's value more highly than your competitor's. In short, you must be able to **outperform** the competition at every turn.

So whether you've studied interior design or not, forgive me for saying it, but you need to be trained properly. I know I'm being repetitive, but that should just tell you how important this training is to your future. Don't make the mistake of assuming that you already know everything there is to know about design or rearrangement design because you've taken a course, read a book or two, collected decorating magazines and so forth. You may know a lot - but we are ALL creatures who FORGET.

It will be impossible for you to offer a greater service to your clients than your competitors if you are not totally, totally immersed in the concepts of arrangement design. If you do less than become an "expert", you are cheating your clients and you will be giving the whole industry a bad rap! Because it's so important, please review Chapter Eighteen for good resources.

NOTE: Knowing and practicing Feng Shui is not considered compatible with solid, generally accepted interior design concepts and techniques. Don't get mad at me and write me nasty email. FS is a totally different philosophy based on strategies that don't necessarily emphasize function and beauty as primary considerations, so be aware. Whether you are a practicing FS consultant or not you should know the basic American interior design concepts and philosophies.

But back to our discussion on marketing your business . . . in short, you must be able to outperform the competition at every turn -- as a designer and as a marketer.

Questions You Must Answer

Allow me to ask you some penetrating questions:

1. How focused are you and how certain are you of your business-marketing strategy?
2. Are you a prototype of innovative strategic marketing winners in the future or an old fashioned tactical marketing dinosaur or a neophyte beginner?
3. There are an infinite number of choices and challenges strategic marketers must consider in turbulent markets and economies such as we have today. How many different scenarios, factors, threats and alternatives have you actually carefully examined and evaluated lately?
4. Your business and marketing strategy should specify exactly how your business intends to successfully compete in the design market. What does your current strategy (or the lack of one) say about you?
5. Your business and marketing strategy should provide the conceptual "glue" that gives shared meaning to all the separate marketing activities and programs you intend to utilize. How cohesive and strong is the marketing statement your current strategy makes?
6. Your strategy must be straightforward in its intent, direction and integrated action. How clear and focused is yours?

Four Key Factors

Your Marketing Strategy Should Be a Function of Four Key Factors:

1. The arena you compete in
2. The "advantage" or positioning theme that differentiates your business from the competition within that arena

3. Access. What communication, media and distribution channels you employ and deploy to get across your "advantage" or positioning theme
4. Activity. The scope and scale of marketing actions to be systematically and sequentially performed in the media and distribution channels you employ.

These choices are highly interdependent. Alter one and you must revise the other three elements of your overall strategy. Have you ever given thought to any of them already? Have you before realized the necessity of integrating them all together into a seamless united whole? If you really and truly want to be amazingly successful in this business, or any business, then you have some serious thinking to do first.

The best time to do this is now. In the beginning. Don't wait until competition takes over your market to examine and develop new opportunities, approaches, positioning and advantages. You can't wait to examine new products or services or opportunities. And you can't wait until you start losing business to try to build business.

So I hope you can see by now that finding the right growth strategy for you requires a very well thought out strategic marketing plan - one that does not diffuse your resources, opportunities, time or health. You need to choose the best combination of tactics, weave them together into an overall strategy, while minimizing risk, waste and ineffectiveness.

Without a clear, integrated, WRITTEN goal-based Super Strategy and vision for your design business, your company is likely to be reactive in its current actions, and aimless in pursuing future growth directions or activities. Not only that, but it requires an ability to see the marketing and competitive forces operating in your part of the country - and be able to predict how they will most likely change, react and evolve in response to the competitive threat YOU will bring to the forefront.

By systematically focusing dedicated attention to these issues and continuously searching for new and better ways to strategically gain competitive marketing advantages - the outcome you desire will be fully and quickly achieved.

Provide Value for Your Clients

"There is only one valid definition of a business' purpose: to create a satisfied customer." (Peter Drucker) It is your clients who will ultimately determine what your business is or isn't and how successful and prosperous you thereby become. A masterful marketing strategy is a clear, certain statement of direction, purpose, objectives and outcome your business confidently expects to achieve.

The acid test of your strategic marketing plan is whether or not it will deliver and sustain a decisive competitive advantage for your company. It's really that simple and basic. Remember, I said "sustainable". Therefore, you need to know the answers to the following eight questions:

1. How do YOU currently evaluate marketing tactics like advertising or promotional effectiveness?
2. Does your current marketing approach stress product leadership, service leadership, customer leadership or brand leadership? Or does it stress nothing?
3. Can you clearly define your value proposition?
4. Do you use strategic marketing to continually move your sales up the "value ladder"?

5. How thoroughly have you assessed and utilized your tangible, intangible and knowledge-based marketing assets?
6. How many new products or services have you or will you strategically introduce in the next 18 months?
7. How many new markets or selling systems have you gone after strategically?
8. Have you developed a formalized, written marketing growth strategy?

The Answers Are Not "Hidden" -
But You Need to Look Outside of Design to Find Them

Master looking outside your business to sense critical changes, trends, threats and opportunities - then thoroughly analyze each of these situations or conditions to develop the best strategic options to pursue. So how do you best do it? First your business needs to build a forward-looking, ultra competitive marketing strategy that effectively specifies EXACTLY how your business intends to successfully compete in the interior redesign industry.

Whatever you settle on, it must be all of these: 1) sustainable, 2) preemptive, 3) preeminent. You have to be able to produce a sustainable competitive advantage that you can predict! If you can't do that, it's not a strategy you should be following. You need to arrive at a point where you can predict, with reasonable certainty, what the outcome of your concepts, offers and such will be.

Do you know what the end result is that you want for your business? If you don't know where you want to go, how will you get there? You must know what your final destination is to be. And after you have settled on a destination, ask yourself if it is the best and highest destination you are capable of achieving? Don't sell yourself short.

You'll never be able to achieve your own Super Strategy unless and until you first examine and carefully evaluate the best performing tactical options, opportunities and marketing alternatives "OUT THERE", so you can grasp what kind of strategic visions and goals are truly possible.

Frequently, when you approach the creation of a marketing strategy from this mindset, you dramatically increase your sights on how much more is really possible from the same effort, investment, staff (if any), opportunity, cost and time. Without critical thinking, sequential activities, systematic execution and implementation - little gets accomplished.

You need to be able to accurately predict how your marketing strategies will most likely change, respond and evolve to the new actions you will take. And even further, you need to be able to accurately predict the responses of your competition and the marketplace. Does this sound impossible? Overwhelming? Well, you wouldn't be alone if you felt that way. That's why you have to have a near-obsessive commitment to winning! This is what it takes to make the difference between mediocrity and huge profits.

Not every one has that kind of commitment to winning. I recently invited my sister to revisit my website and take a look at the list of free tips links on my sitemap. She was blown away. Over time, she had no idea that my site had grown so vastly from it's fledgling beginnings. But she doesn't realize that I've only just begun and am still a long way from the place I intend to be. She commented that she would never have the time to read everything I have there now. That's ok. I never intended for any single person to read every single page on the site. It's there for them should they need it, but it was designed for quite a different purpose.

You see, I have a Super Strategy at work and my free tips pages are only one tactical part of that overall strategy. I commit time every month to building that part of my plan, but it is only one part of the strategy. It has it's purpose and place, but it will not, by itself, even begin to accomplish the goals I have set for my business. It is my Super Strategy that will accomplish that.

So the first step in your successful marketing strategy development is to determine the basic strategy you want to successfully mount and the reason why you think it represents the best possible approach for your business objectives.

Truly world-class strategic marketing is only possible when your products, services, markets, current selling systems, competition and market opportunities have been clearly and accurately defined.

To help you recognize a number of critical elements that heavily influence what kind of strategy you should be using, write down the answers to these questions:

1. What is your selling proposition going to be and why?
2. What's your front-end acquisition mechanism going to be and why did you choose it?
3. What will your back-end, repurchase offering/series/sequence be and, again why did you choose that combination or order?
4. Do you know what your allowable acquisition cost, incremental profit contribution and cost per lead/ customer or product sale is?
5. What's your repurchase rate, retention rate and attrition rate?
6. What's the need you are either creating or filling and how will/are you doing it better or more appealingly than your competition?
7. How many methods of creative marketing success are you incorporating?
8. How many applications for growing your business are you going to be using and why?
9. How are you building an edge against the competition?
10. What are you doing to establish and sustain credibility and trust?
11. Do you create all your marketing with the end result clearly in mind?
12. Does your marketing have true "flow" and strong value appeal to your prospective customer?
13. Do you know how to effectively evaluate advertising and direct mail?
14. Are you collecting sales copy, sales letters, advertising examples from other industries that have been successful and studying them?
15. Have you implemented a criteria chart that all your ideas must pass before being employed as a tactic?
16. Do you understand the lifetime value of a customer and know how much you can expect to profit from each customer?
17. What system have you implemented that will get your present clients to purchase more from you more often?
18. Do you understand the economics of strategic marketing?

Your business has to create more value in your customer's mind. If you do that successfully, you will experience infinitely greater growth and profitability for your redesign business. I am always seeking ways to increase the value of my products and services. This entire treatise on the subject of Super Strategies is just one segment of that process. You see, originally this part of your training was not included in earlier versions. I have added it now to make the whole experience more valuable to you, my readers. I know it's complicated and you may not understand much of it upon first reading it. So you should read it several times and take notes. It will become more clear as you digest it more thoroughly. It will really become clear as you start to implement some of it and test the waters and try it out.

Yes, it's more work than you want to do right now. But it's totally up to you to decide at what level of success you wish to be. And that goes for anything and everything in life. I'm trying to teach you marketing's greatest single contribution to business! **It gives you knowledge of how you can best leverage UP all your opportunities, efforts, assets, capital, people and activities.**

And once you have made your decisions and begun to implement them, it then becomes necessary to set up a system that will help you analyze what you are doing. You will need to continuously evaluate, measure, monitor, quantify and improve every single tactic you put to use. By doing this your overall strategy will be tweaked and tweaked again, until you find the core system that functions optimally. And even after you achieve that, you will want to continually adapt everything you are doing to the constantly changing marketplace and the tactics employed by your competition. So it's a never ending process. But that's what makes it both fun and challenging.

Four Major Strategy Options

There are four major ways a strategy can be built: 1) Product Leadership; 2) Service Leadership; 3) Customer Leadership; and 4) Brand Leadership. Which one will you pick?

Don't let this sound too complex to you. You just need help recognizing all the underlying forces that competitively impact or influence your business performance, profitability and success.

So let's give you some specific things to do:

- You need to cultivate a framework for effectively predicting competitor behavior. So study what your competition is doing. Look at their advertising: websites, yellow page advertising, flyers, brochures, sales pitches, etc.
- You need to better comprehend the vital links between how profit is created, maximized and sustained. How are you getting your qualified prospects to hire you, how are you getting each client to utilize your services to the maximum and getting you a good supply of referrals to sustain your business.
- You need to totally rethink your past ideas on what competition and competing to win really means. Is it always an adversarial thing or could there be some friendly cooperation that benefits both parties?
- You need to be able to better assess the design industry, understand your competitor's positions, and search for alternative means for filling the needs of your customers.
- You need to choose a competitive position that gives you the greatest advantage - but it needs to be an advantage that you can sustain over the life of your business.
- You need to bring a disciplined, integrated structure to your business if you want to grow it into something superior.
- You need to adopt a far more sophisticated view of competition that surpasses those around you.

What I'm really saying, to put it bluntly, is that you need to become a world-class strategic marketer if you want to make it to the big time. This will not happen overnight. It takes time. It takes willingness to read, study and analyze what other people are doing that has made them successful. It takes hard work.

Your challenge from this day forward must, therefore, become identifying what advantages exist and incorporating as many as possible into the centerpiece of all the strategic marketing you ever do. You need to think differently. Little by little you will start thinking continuously along the lines of how to achieve greater market penetration, product expansion, market expansion, diversification, brand equity and much, much more. You'll start seeing economic uncertainty as a key opportunity, not a detriment. You'll evaluate many more marketing scenarios than you ever expected to do in your life. You will learn.

Best of all, you'll eventually create a battle-tested blueprint approach for taking your products, services and entire business and transforming it all into greater perceived value in your marketplace. That will be great for your clients!

You'll be able to answer questions like these:

- Which markets offer me the best opportunities for most profitable growth?
- What do my target customers really need or want?
- What mix of channels, partners will help me reach and sell to the most desirable group of clients at the lowest marketing and selling costs possible?
- Do I offer the right products/services or solutions - and if not what should I be offering?
- Do I have a compelling value proposition?
- What would make the message even more appealing?

Yeah! It's a learning process. And those that are willing to tackle it will go on to be hugely profitable and wildly successful. And those that want to cringe and run away right now, claim it is too hard and too much work, will no doubt end up failing, or at best only marginally successful. So at this point, you are faced with a decision. You can do nothing. You can market your design services in a purely tactical way, lose ground every year, and operate strictly on a reactive basis and cross your fingers and hope for the best.

Or you can go back and re-read this entire section two more times, taking notes. And after you have done that, you can choose to begin to attack your business strategy with a whole new attitude and direction. If you choose the latter, you will not stop learning here. You will seek to learn as much about marketing as you can from other books and courses, from studying the sales materials you get in the mail that "sell you". You will go online and study the sales letters and marketing strategies of businesses from every conceivable segment, including those in the redesign and traditional design industry. You will teach yourself to look at the possibilities and then you will put them into practice.

A Word About Seminars and Classes

You may already be aware of many seminars for interior redesign and home staging sprinkled around the country. Some are good and others are very poor. What you may not realize at first glance is that people usually only retain about 10% of what they hear at a seminar. Many times the gathering is disruptive. Many times attendees don't get along. I've even heard of the trainers getting into fights in the middle of the seminar when co-teaching. So you just never know what you're going to get until it's too late.

The number of homes advertised to be redesigned, as part of the seminar, rarely materialize. To make matters worse, students are often assigned just one room in the home and "teamed" with one or more additional students to that room. So you might not get to work independently.

Arguments can ensue between those redesigning one room and those doing another room in the same home, because each "team" wants some of the same furniture and accessories for the room they are working on as another "team". While there are situations that progress harmoniously, there are many situations in which students have been severely disappointed by bickering and hostilities.

Seminars for this industry usually range in price from $2500-$3500. And that doesn't include one's airfare and lodging for the duration of the seminar. Not to mention the hardship on family members who are left to fend on their own while you are away.

This was one of the main reasons why, in 2002, I was the first trainer to offer books and a home study course for the industry. They said it couldn't be taught this way. Naturally that proved to be untrue.

Today thousands and thousands of entrepreneurs have learned from the privacy of their home how to do both interior redesign and home staging. I am very pleased to have been the catalyst to bring about such change, making the learning process much more affordable, much more flexible and much more comprehensive at the same time.

My philosophy is to give great training, but at the same time to minimize your investment for training so that you can put your dollars into marketing and promoting your business. I want you to recoup your training investment as quickly as possible.

So that's another reason why a home study course is so advantageous over seminars.

In our courses, we literally load you up with a small library of manuals, and actual marketing tools that will do much of the promotional work for you. These courses and tools have worked magic for others who have gone on to stellar careers.

If you have already purchased an individual book or books, we are willing to give you credit or substitution for upgrading to a course. But this is a case by case basis, so you'll need to contact us and discuss your options with us personally. For more information, call (714) 963-3071. Office hours are Monday-Friday, 9:00-5:00 Pacific Standard Time.

Chapter Fifteen (Bonus)

The Secret Art of Hanging Art

Introduction

My associate and I have been installing art work since 1983 throughout California – from my office in Huntington Beach to San Francisco and as far south as San Diego and east to Palm Springs. My associate and I have hung thousands of framed art images in small businesses, large corporations, hotels, restaurants, hospitals and private residences. (I guess you could say I definitely have a lot of "hang-ups"!)

In all these years, I have never had a client call me and report that a piece I had hung had fallen from the wall or had any installation problem. I share this information, so that you will know I have experienced every type of situation you could possibly encounter, and I hope to alleviate any potential anxiety or frustration you might have. If you don't know of a professional installer or don't want to spend the money to hire one, this information will help you do it yourself with confidence.

For those of you who aren't that concerned about hanging something in a professional manner (i.e. you're a student and you have in your dorm room an unframed poster, taped or pinned to the wall and you don't care if it's crooked or not), I hope you'll take the time to read this section anyway, or print off a copy to keep for the future, because the time will undoubtedly come when you will care about what you're hanging and you're going to want to do it right.

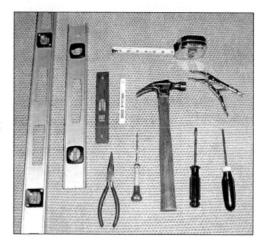

This report is going to help you do it right the first time, so that you don't wind up with numerous holes in the wall back of the artwork on your newly painted, paneled or wallpapered wall. To that end, there are 3 basic rules for a successful installation:

EDUCATION (read this section in it's entirety before you begin);
EQUIPMENT (have the proper tools to accomplish the job);
ENJOYMENT (enjoy the challenge and the journey).

Tools

Like most every other task in life, having the right tools makes most jobs fairly easy – whereas having the wrong tools or no tools at all, makes the job difficult and frustrating. Here's a list of what you should consider acquiring.

Hammer -- If you do not have one readily available, you might pick up a new one when you go to a hardware store to get the other tools you probably don't have. Choose one that is comfortable for you.

Carpenter's Level -- (2 sizes recommended) 48" and 18" (shown on left in photo, prior page)

Plummer's Level:(2 sizes recommended) 8" and 5" (shown near left, prior page)

Needle Nose Plier (bottom center, prior page)

25' Metal Measuring Tape (shown at top)

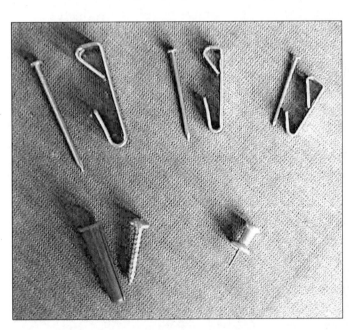

Locking Pliers (toward top right) and Needle Nose or Regular Pliers (bottom left)

Screw Drivers -- Phillips and straight (bottom right)

Scratch Awl (middle bottom) or Electric Drill (not shown)

Pictured to the left are: hanging hooks in 3 sizes along the top; red plastic screw anchor with screw (left bottom); push pin (bottom right).

Choose a hook that is appropriate for the size and weight of what you are going to hang. I like using two hooks for wire to help keep the art work level.

While you may not need all of the above tools and hardware for your project, it's a good idea, if you can, to get everything you think you might need in advance, because you never know when you might have a project that requires them.

The Latest in Hardware

Many companies offer the traditional j-shaped picture hangers pictured here (left). These are great for drywall or sheet rock, depending on where you live. They are very inexpensive. Impex Industrial Hardware (Miami) has taken it a step further.

If you've ever tried to remove hooks and had trouble, Impex has nails with a knurled head that are easy to grip and remove.

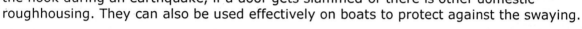

Then there's the new Art Guard security hanger, also called Tremor Hangers or Kid Safe Hangers (right). The picture wire snaps under a spring that safeguards the artwork from sliding off the hook during an earthquake, if a door gets slammed or there is other domestic roughhousing. They can also be used effectively on boats to protect against the swaying.

Everstraight Hanging System of Fort Colins, CO has a plastic picture hanger that can be used with hanging wire, saw tooth hangers, anchors or interlocked with another Everstraight hanger, promising perfectly straight pictures without the use of a leveling device. The hangers come in 1", 3", 5" and 7" sizes and will support objects up to 75 lbs. and 48" wide, they say.

Magnet Energy Collection from Danion Industries of Boca Raton, FL, has this hook on the left. The hook features -- yes -- a magnet that guides the picture wire into place without the awkward, reach-around-blindly, strain your shoulder maneuver that we've all tried. The top of the hanger is angled, and a hardened steel nail rests in a recessed area when hammered into place. Unlike other hangers, this one has no surface upon which the wire can get caught, except the hook itself, simply lift the framed picture up to the hook and the wire is attracted by the magnet and guided into place. YES!

Tests, they say, show that the smaller one will hold up to 50 lbs, while the larger one will hold up to 160 lbs. on a single hanger. You could also use wood screws, sheet metal screws or generic hollow wall anchors rather than a nail if you choose.

The Hercules Hooks (next page) are very innovative in that you can use them without tools and simply "push" the point on one end into your drywall and hang up your art. You can find these at any hardware store or even order them from Amazon.Com. They come in packs and are quite reasonably priced.

Preparation

Since most homes now have drywall, let's first start with a brief explanation of what to do to cover holes that already exist so that your finished arrangement will look perfect.

FOR PINHOLES

Get some joint compound (spackle) and press some into and over the hole with a putty knife. Use the putty knife to smooth the excess out, trying to blend it with the wall. When it is dry, sand it lightly to blend and smooth. Repaint if necessary.

FOR LARGE HOLES
Cut a piece of pegboard slightly larger than the hole. Even though slightly larger, you must be able to push it into the hole, so make sure it is not too much larger. This will serve as the backing for the patch. Before putting in the hole, slip a piece of wire through two of the holes in the pegboard, going in one hole and coming out another one so that you have the two ends on one side. Smear compound or spackle around the edges of the pegboard and while wet, press the pegboard into the hole using the wire to keep from pressing it too far in. Try to align the pegboard so that it is very slightly depressed into the hole. Now take the wire and wrap the ends around a pencil and turn the pencil to the right or left. This will cause a slight shift of the pegboard in the hole. This shift, together with the compound, will serve to hold the patch tightly in place. Allow the compound to dry. When the patch has completely dried, cut the wire off and fill the recessed area with compound. Lightly sand the compound after it has dried and blend it with the rest of the wall with a sponge. Repaint.

Laser Level

Recently, as of this writing, a new gadget has come on the market which creates a laser beam on the horizontal or vertical plumb line. One such widget is made by Ryobi (there are others as well) and is available at your favorite hardware store for around $40. The laser head rotates 360 degrees and the laser lens rotates 90 degrees. It will even wrap itself around corners for you. Their laser level has a vacuum base for gripping the wall. Since the laser can shoot at any angle, it's especially great for deciding the exact angle for a wall grouping on your staircase.

Ryobi® introduces the AIRgrip™ laser level that uses patented vacuum technology to affix itself to walls without marring surfaces. Painters, drywallers, carpenters, remodelers and homeowners will find this new laser level easy to use and especially helpful. The AIRgrip™ laser level is perfect for hanging chair-rail, stairway railing, aligning pictures, putting up borders, installing crown molding, mounting shelving and leveling electrical outlet rough-ins.

"Our new AIRgrip Laser Level lets you hang paintings on expensive wallpaper or put up chair rail on your custom paneling," said Jeff Dils, President, Power Tool Group, TTI North America, "and you don't have to puncture what's priceless just to get a level."

The AIRgrip™ laser level uses a small battery-powered motor to create a vacuum on the bottom of a rubber base so that it can stick to painted walls, untreated drywall, most wall paper and many other non-porous surfaces. Unlike devices which use pins, nails or expensive adhesive tapes, the AIRgrip™ laser level will not leave a single mark on a wall, yet is powerful enough to adhere both vertically or horizontally for several hours at a time.

The laser light's 635 nm laser diode provides a visible light for up to 30 feet. The 360-degree rotating head offers users multiple angle capabilities, while a unique rotating laser head rotates 90 degrees for vertical and horizontal applications.

A special carrying case comes with a multi-purpose base, a Velcro strap for securing the unit to cylindrical objects and 2-by-4's, push pins for applying level to uneven surfaces, a standard tripod mounting fixture and 2 AA batteries.

Installation

Word of Caution

Works of art, mirrors, shelves and other types of wall mounted decorative pieces carry a financial and, sometimes an emotional, value. They are also most likely to have glass or the art itself may be breakable, so be sure to take every precaution to hang each piece safely and securely to protect it from becoming dislodged and being damaged and/or causing injury. Be sure to pick up all tools, hooks, push pins, nails and anything else you used to work with when you are done. Check your carpet and floors thoroughly. Push pins and nails "hidden" in carpeting can be dangerous.

To help you stay organized, consider buying a case to keep everything together. I use clear plastic bags with self sealers to separate my hooks and nails and screws. My push pins go in a small clear hard plastic box. As I work, I make a habit of always putting my tools back in their specified compartments in my tool kit so I will always know where to find them, and to prevent accidents.

Selecting the Location

Some designers say you should never hang anything on a narrow panel of wall, say anything less than 3 feet wide. But this is a hard rule that doesn't take into consideration the uniqueness of each room, the available wall space and the style, colors, patterns of the room. Nor does it account for the architectural elements in the room. Last week we rearranged the furniture in a client's home who only had one 2 foot panel of wall between two large interior "window" openings. Since it was the only "wall" in the entry, it would be appropriate to hang something on it, even though it was narrow.

But since the wall over a sofa is one of the most commonly decorated walls in a room, we will use that as our primary example.

For illustration purposes, let's say that you have a large, horizontally formatted image which you have elected to hang over your sofa. For the best scale with the sofa, please note that the art image (framed) should be approximately 2/3rds the width of the sofa. Any measurement that strays too far from the 2/3rds rule runs the risk of being overly large for the sofa or way too small, thus feeling "lost" on the wall.

If you adhere closely to the following measurements, you're always going to have a single art image or a grouping of images that is in proper scale to the sofa: 2:3, 3:5, 4:6, and 5:7. You can go a little below or a little over but use this as a guide and you can't go wrong. (If you don't have a single piece that comes close to this ratio, then put two or three smaller images together as a grouping.)

You're going to want to place the artwork so that there is approximately 6-8 inches or a hand span between the top of the sofa and the base of the framed artwork. Why 6-8 inches? Because if you place it higher on the wall, the eye will be drawn to the gap between the art and the sofa. This is not good. The eye could also be drawn toward the ceiling, rather than into the furniture arrangement. This is also not good. The only exception to this rule would come if the image is extremely large, very bold or active. You might want to "cheat" a little so that the image doesn't appear as if it is about to fall behind the sofa.

In addition to that, every good art image has a focal point. If the focal point is high in the image, the eye will be drawn upwards with greater ease than if the focal point is placed low in the image. You definitely want the eye of the viewer to remain within the image and then moving down into the furniture arrangement, so be careful that you don't hang the artwork too far above the sofa.

Don't worry about people hitting the back of their head on the art if it is hung close to the sofa. It's just not going to happen if the sofa or chair has a fairly thick back.

Finding the Right Measurement

The key to easy and professional art installation is accurate measurement! The whole point is to determine where you will place the hook and it's as simple as that!

Horizontal measurement: Find the center horizontal point of the sofa, and if you're hanging a single piece of art, locate the center of the horizontal measurement of the art. Place a push pin in the wall slightly below the top of the sofa to locate the center of the sofa. By placing the push pin below the top of the sofa, the tiny hole will not show after the art is actually hung. Another way to hide the push pin hole is to place it above where you estimate the bottom of the art will be.

Vertical measurement: The easiest way at this point is to have an assistant. Have your assistant hold the art up against the wall, approximately 6" or so from the top of the sofa. Stand back and determine where you feel it looks best from that height. You'll have to decide quickly as your assistant won't be able to hold the art up very long, especially if it is large.

If the art, mat and frame are very dark, you'll probably want to put a little extra space between the art's base and the sofa, due to the "weight" the art will appear to have. You don't want it to feel, after hung, as if it is about to fall down behind the sofa. Sometimes very light or very bright artwork has the same effect.

The main thing to remember is that you want the artwork to feel part of a larger grouping, including your sofa, end tables and so forth. So place it so it is a definite part of the grouping, but not so close to the sofa as to appear that it might be about to fall behind it.

Now, while your assistant is holding the art over the sofa, take a push pin and place it in the wall about ¼" below the top of the frame. You don't want this pin hole to show later, so place it slightly lower, and try to get it as close to the horizontal center of the art as possible.

If you don't have anyone to hold the art in place while you get a good visual of the appropriate height, and the art is not too heavy, try to hold it up yourself following the above measuring rules. But if the art is heavy, then take your metal measuring tape and lock it to match the vertical height of the art. Hold the measuring tape against the wall with the lower end of the tape approximately 6" from the top of the sofa. Place a push pin in the wall approximately ¼" below the top end of the measuring tape and as close to the center you've already marked with a previous push pin.

Move the pin you used to mark the horizontal center of the wall to indicate the base of the artwork. Stand back from the sofa and try to focus on the top and bottom push pin and see if your eye might be drawn to the space between the bottom pin and the sofa. If so, consider hanging the art a little closer to the sofa. If not, you can be reasonably sure that you have chosen the right height for the art.

When in doubt, always hang something lower rather than higher. You can always move it up without a hole showing, but if you start out with it too high, you could have some serious problems that might be a real headache to cover up.

Always remember, when hanging art or anything else over furniture, you should keep the 2/3rds rule in mind for the horizontal measurement, and the base of the largest accessory you are hanging should be approximately 6-8" from the top of the furniture below it. The only exception to this would be if you're hanging something over a piece of furniture that has a shelf or top on which you will be placing other accessories. In that case, you'll probably want to hang the art a little higher to accommodate for the heights of these other accessories.

However, even then, it's a good idea to have some overlapping. If your artwork has mats and a frame, it's perfectly acceptable to keep it hung lower and place other accessories on the top of the furniture in front of it. You can even safely overlap the image, so long as it's not blocking an essential part of the image.

Keep in mind to where the viewer of the artwork is most likely to be. If they are most likely to be seated, you don't want to place art so high on the wall that it cannot be appreciated comfortably. If your location is a "walk-by" wall with no furniture beneath it, the rules change. Art on these walls will be hung higher.

Vertical Height for Walk-by Walls

Forget about eye level. Eye level varies because we are all different heights. The eye level for a 5' person is certainly going to be different than it is for someone 6'5". So you need to consider all of the people that live in the home primarily, not visitors. Having said that, you should know that the universally accepted eye level is 5-1/2 feet (66 inches). So if you are very short or extremely tall, you need to consider the eye level that is universally accepted as being middle of the road and hang your artwork accordingly.

You want to hang all art work so that the main part of the image is easily viewed by most people. And particularly the focal point of the image. Therefore, art that has a high-placed focal point may not need to be hung quite as high as an image where the focal point is lower. Artists usually place the focal point along a diagonal line between one corner and the other, and at a place that is perpendicular to an opposite corner - forming a 90° angle at the diagonal line. They are almost never placed in the middle of the image. So the focal point is more likely to be about a 3rd of the way down from the top, or a 3rd of the way up from the bottom, somewhere along that diagonal line.

This isn't a huge consideration for you to make adjustments by, but it's good to take note of it if you can.

If your height is far above or below the average, you need to hang the artwork according to the average eye level, not yours. If you don't, your will make viewing it really uncomfortable for most people.

Extremely tall people have a tendency to hang art near the ceiling and it definitely looks very funny and odd that high. Extremely short people might have the opposite tendency.

By the way, never hang two companions at different heights unless there is a staircase below creating a diagonal angle. Then follow the same angle when hanging companions (or a grouping). An exception to this is if there is some furniture below that has different heights, again creating an angle of some sort, then it is appropriate to vary the heights of the artwork so that they mirror the angle created by the furniture. In all other cases, hang companions on the same plane (or at the same height). It is awkward for the eye to view, and it's easy to create a feeling of imbalance when you hang companions at different heights for no reason.

Hanging Art That is Wired

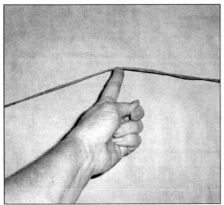

Check the back of your frame to see what kind of hanging device the framer has provided. Generally speaking, except for very small frames or very large ones, the device will be wire, stretched from one side frame to the other side, with some slack in the tension.

Pull the wire upward until it is taut in the center back and measure the distance from the top of the frame to the point where the wire reaches. This simulates the position of the wire once the art has been hung and the weight has pulled the wire taut.

If your measurement from the top of the frame to the wire is, let's say, 7", then measure 6-3/4" down from the push pin that you have already located ¼" down from where you want the top of the frame to hang.

This 6-3/4" measurement is where you're going to place your hook or nail.

NOTE: Be sure to place the BOTTOM of the hook at this point, because this measure is for the place where the wire will hang FROM, and this is not the place where you will nail the hook to the wall. The nail is actually going to go into the wall a little bit higher than this point. This is very important.

After hanging the art on the hook on the wall, you'll want to make it level. Place a small level on the top of the frame. Line up the bubble. If you don't have a level, stand back from the artwork and visually compare the distance from the ceiling to the frame on both sides. Adjust as necessary until it feels and looks level to your eye. Be sure to stand squarely in front of the image to check the level. If you are standing off to one side you will get a lopsided view and your adjustments will not be accurate.

To eliminate glare, consider placing a small piece of cork between the upper center of the frame and the wall, if your art is framed under glass.

Types and Numbers of Hooks

Depending upon the size, and especially the weight, of the framed art, your hooks must be proportionate. Most packaged hooks which you can acquire from any hardware store will specify the recommended weights they can easily handle.

But regardless, I always recommend 2 hooks for medium to large pieces – not just for extra security – but because two hooks help keep the art piece level on the wall. This can be especially advantageous if the art is hung on a wall that also has a door that, when slammed shut, causes the art to shift.

 Sometimes just the gust of air from a door opening or shutting can cause art to shift. Having two hooks holding the art in place really reduces this problem and provides extra security at the same time.

If you elect to use two hooks (recommended), you're going to need an easy way to space them an equal distance from the vertical center. Don't waste your time looking for studs. You don't need studs to hang average sized pictures securely.

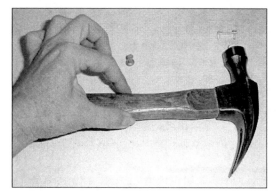

At this point you're going to have to gauge yourself what distance you feel the art needs between the two hooks. It will be totally up to you, based on the horizontal width of what you are hanging. For small pieces, you'll only need a few inches between the two hooks, but for larger images you'll need to spread them further apart. But you're probably never going to need them to be more than one foot to 1-1/2 feet apart.

When placing two hooks, you will also see the artwork hang just a slight bit higher on the wall because of the reduced slack in the wire, so adjust accordingly.

Starting from the vertical measurement equal to the height you want your hooks, measure out half the distance you want to separate the hooks. It doesn't have to be any specific measurement. Approximations are just fine. Place your hammer head under the first hook after you have hung it, and with your fingers mark the approximate distance from the hook to the center, which is indicated by a push pin. Then move your hammer head to the center spot, and place your second hook where your fingers and thumb are holding the hammer handle. This is the quick and easy way. If you want it precise, use your measuring tape to get an exact measurement. But it's not really that essential, unless you're doing some close and tight measurements for a wall grouping and you really want to be very precise.

Using Screw Anchors

Most of the time you will not need to use screw anchors. I prefer not to use them because they, if removed, leave a larger hole in the wall and are very difficult to remove. If you don't get the screw in right the first time, you might ruin the anchor and then you have a real problem.

So I basically only use screw anchors when I am doing a security installation, generally not in a residence, or if I am hanging something, like a plant, from the ceiling - or exceptionally heavy pieces, such as oversized art or mirrors. (One of the advantages of using anchors is you can install heavy pieces in drywall – not needing to find wall studs.)

After locating the place where I wish to put the anchor, I use a scratch awl to start the hole. I place the scratch awl where I want the hole and use my hammer to pound the awl partly into the wall. Since my scratch awl is slightly smaller in diameter than the screw anchor I usually use, I have to turn it around in the hole a few times to slightly enlarge the hole. By doing this, the anchor is relatively easy to pound into the hole and you are less likely to damage it in the process. But be careful that you don't make the hole too large. Then the anchor will not be snug and it will not properly hold the screw.

Then screw in the appropriately sized screw, upon which you will hang the art or mirror. Always use two screws for heavy items.

Hanging Oversized Art or Mirrors

Oversized art images and large mirrors generally do not come wired. This is due to the extra weight. So usually framers will attach a metal hanging device to each vertical side of the frame. This puts less strain on the frame and makes the installation more secure than if using wire.

When hanging one of these pieces, measure down the distance from the top of the frame to the top of the hanger. Make sure the distance is the same on both sides. If it is not, move one of the hangers so that it is even with the other one or simply adjust your measurement.

If the measurements are the same, then you are fine. However, if the measurements are NOT the same, pay particular note to the following.

NOTE: Be sure to remember when you are taking these two measurements on the back of the frame, that the left and right measurements will be REVERSED when you turn the picture around to hang it on the wall. So the right measurement is for the left side on the wall and the left measurement is for the right side on the wall.

After you have taken these measurements (and its a good idea to write them down), you now need to take very accurate measurements of the distance horizontally between the hanging devices.

Be sure to measure the distance from the MID POINT of one hanger to the MID POINT of the other hanger. The mid point is where your hanger will connect with the hook. The hook needs to be placed so that it will connect with the hanger right in the middle. So it is a good idea to measure this distance very carefully and double check your measurements BEFORE you nail the hooks into the wall – this will insure you that the hangers on the frame will precisely line up with the hooks in the wall.

At this point, you need to establish how high the picture or mirror is going to hang. Follow the same rules listed above in locating the proper height. However, this time, once you have placed the first push pin into the wall 1/4" below where you want the top of the frame to hang, you're going to need to locate where the two hooks will be placed.

Since you want these hooks to be level, you first need to establish two level pins to guide all your other measurements. This is where you're going to need your 48" level (mentioned in the Tools section above).

Measure down from your center pin to the distance of where the hangers are (the distance from the top of the frame to the top of each hanger). Remember to subtract 1/4" from this measurement. Move your center push pin to that lower position.

Take your horizontal measurement (the distance between the mid point of both hangers) and divide it by two. Start with the center push pin that you have already re-located, and measure out from that pin, using the 1/2 measurement. Locate a second push pin as close to the vertical height of the center pin as you can. Then use your level to make sure that the 2nd push pin is exactly level with the center pin. Do the same thing on the other side of the center pin.

To double check your levels, place your level on top of the two outer pins, having first removed the center pin. If they are not completely level, adjust one or the other until your level indicates they are perfectly placed. Double check the horizontal measurement to make sure they will line up perfectly with the two hangers on the back of the frame.

If you are working with a double-sized image and the hangers are farther than 48" apart, you'll have to just go with your 1/2 distance levels. Remember, when the hangers are not the same distance from the top of the frame, you need to reverse your measurements on the wall. Also remember, when hanging your hooks, you need to place the bottom of the hook at the hole where your pin was so that it will connect with a hanger at the right height.

Attach both hooks to the wall and you're ready to hang the picture or mirror. Find an assistant to help you lift it and make sure that each hanger is securely hung on the hook. Check and double check this step.

Step back from the picture or mirror and focus on the top frame to make sure that it is completely level. Double check the level by placing a level on the top of the frame.

Consider using D-hooks and L-screws for very large pieces for a secure hold.

Hanging Companions

As I explained earlier, always hang companions at the same height unless over stairs or over a furniture grouping that creates an angular line at the top of the furniture. If one or both of the images are directional (let's say a figure is facing left in one and right in the other one), place them so that the figures face into the grouping and not out of it. In other words, a figure facing right should hang on the left side so that the figure is looking into the middle of the grouping.

Don't hang companions together if one is visually much stronger than the other by it's color, it's color value or some other difference. Images that differ greatly in their overall visual strength will not look good hung as companions. One will overpower the other one and create an imbalanced feeling. Many artists created companion images that are meant to be hung as a pair. This is ideal.

Depending on the size of each piece, you're going to want to leave about 4-8" of space between the two pieces. Don't hang them too close where they feel crowded together. But by the same token, don't hang them so far apart that they lose the feeling of being a united whole.

Horizontal Measurement

First, locate the center point on the wall where the two companions will hang. Place a push pin in the wall at approximately the height you'll want them to hang. Then hold, or have your assistant hold, one of the companions (let's say the "left" piece), up against the wall 3 or 4 inches to the left of the center-point push pin. Visually determine the height you want -- moving the piece up or down until satisfied. Place a push pin at the approximate mid-point of the top of the piece at 1/4" below the top.

Then adjust the height of your center-point push pin -- using a level to make sure they are both the same height.

Now measure the width of the piece itself. Divide that horizontal measurement by 2 and add half the distance you have decided to put between the two frames.

Let's say that the width is 24" and you are going to hang the two images about 6" apart. Half of 24" is 12", plus half of 6" is 3". 12" + 3" = 15".

Now you can be specific and adjust, if necessary, your location of your push pin, marking the height and approximate horizontal distance between the two push pins you have in the wall. The pin marking the mid-point of your image should be 15" to the left of your center point pin. Make whatever adjustments necessary and in doing so, once you have the mid-point pin precisely 15" from the center pin, double check your height by using your level and make any adjustments necessary.

Next measure 15" from the center point pin toward the right and place your 3rd (right-side) pin at that distance at approximately the same height. Use your level and adjust your height.

Remember -- when adjusting your height for the 2nd piece, adjust the 3rd pin -- do not move your center-point pin -- this would throw off it's level position with the left-side pin. Once the pins are level, double check your 15" distance, making necessary adjustments.

Next in this process of finding out where to put the hooks in the wall, having dealt with the horizontal measurements, we'll now turn to the vertical measurements.

Vertical Measurement

Measure the vertical distance from the top of the frame of one of the pieces to the mid point of the wire after it is pulled upward (until taut). Measure the other one in the same manner to see if the measurement is the same or not. You're in luck if the measurements are the same. If not the same, you'll have to make adjustments on the second piece so that when hung it is at the same height as the first.

Once you have your vertical distance from the top of the frame to the taut wire, you are ready to begin. Take the vertical measurement you have just taken from the image you are going to hang first. Move the mid-point pin down that distance. This will be the mark that you will use to hang that image -- the left-side image. Now repeat this for the right-side image.

Next nail your hooks to the wall with the bottom of the hook located at the hole that the pin made in the wall.

If the vertical measurement from the top of the frame to the taut wire on both images is exactly the same, it will be quite easy for you to double check height by placing your level on the hooks, making sure your heights are the same.

Hang the images on the hooks. Using a small level, make sure each piece is level.

Step back and visually check the heights of both images. You can also check the height level by placing a level on the two corners in the middle of the grouping to make sure they are hanging at the same height.

If you find the second image is slight higher or lower than the first, you can pull out the hook for the second image and move it up or down accordingly. This is usually a step you can just do by eyeing it, without having to take measurements.

An alternate way to hang companions is to take craft paper or newspaper taped together and trace around the arrangement on the floor. Tape the paper to the wall after marking on the paper where the hooks should go. Align your hooks and nail them into the wall. Then remove the paper and hang your pictures. You can decide which method is easiest for you.

Hanging a Wall Grouping

Wall groupings are more intricate to hang and therefore take more time, but there's no reason why you cannot be successful. First select the wall you are going to decorate. For the best visual impact, try to group similar artwork together, such as black and white photographs. Do not try to mix color photos with black and white. The more elements that are repeated, the more unity your grouping will have. You can unify a grouping by having all of the art matted and framed the same.

For very small images, consider over-matting them to make them bigger. Or place all of them inside one larger frame so that they do not feel dwarfed on the wall.

Also consider the architectural shapes of your walls, particularly if considering an extremely large grouping or a gallery wall. If you have a cathedral ceiling and the shape of the wall is "triangular", it may be good to follow that same format and create a grouping whose outer shape is triangular, following the same angle as the ceiling. It's important to always remember that a wall grouping should have some outer geometric shape: rectangular, oval, square, circular, triangular. The individual elements in the grouping should be hung close enough together so that when you stand back and view all of them together, you can see the outer geometric shape they have formed together.

For best unity, there should also be some kind of "grid" pattern formed between the individual pieces. Large gaps in the grid will draw unnecessary attention, so if you see gaps of wall between pieces, consider placing smaller pieces inside the gaps to "fill" the "hole". Try to keep the "grid" somewhere between 2-4" wide, but generally no wider, otherwise the individual images lose relationship to each other and the grouping will start to feel disjointed. Keep unity by hanging them close to each other.

Select all of the various elements that will make up the wall grouping, making sure that you have designed a grouping that will be pleasing on the wall. Eliminate any element from the grouping that attracts too much attention to itself. This will not be very appealing. Here again, odd numbers just seem to work best. For large groupings, 9 individual pieces is a very good number to work with -- it just seems to come out and there's usually just enough size and format differences to allow a great deal of flexibility. You can arrange them casually in a very informal group, or you could do three stacks of 3, or 5 on the bottom and 4 on top.

To check the overall balance, tape the imaginary vertical and horizontal axis on the floor. Lay each piece in its chosen spot. Then check each of the four quadrants to make sure that each has sufficient amount of imagery filling it and no single quadrant is stronger visually than another. Squint. Look at the overall grouping on the floor. When you squint, the softer colors seem to almost drop from your vision, leaving you with the stronger, darker colors. Check to make sure that the strongest colors in your overall grouping are well distributed over all four quadrants. You will then have perfect balance.

If there is no furniture placed against the wall, design a grouping whose outside dimensions covers approximately 2/3rds of the wall horizontally. It will be in good proportion to the wall then. If you stray too far below that measurement with the outside dimensions of the grouping, it will tend to feel swallowed up by the wall - kind of lost - and viewers will be drawn to the blank space around the grouping. Exceeding the 2/3rds measurement will place you in a position where the grouping may feel crowded in. It needs to have sufficient "border" to feel perfect once hung. Allowing too little border is unappealing.

Lay the grouping out on the floor in front of the wall where it will hang. Try to adjust the spacing between each individual piece so that there is equal distance from one piece to another. The spacing within a properly designed grouping will form a grid of sorts.

Since this chapter deals with "hanging" art and not with the design of groupings, I will not deal with the specific design concepts that go into designing an appealing wall grouping. If you need help in this area, consider ordering a copy of "Where There's a Wall -- There's a Way" or "Wall Groupings!" (the new replacement book). See the last chapter for details.

Now there are two ways to actually hang the grouping. In the first method, you start with the anchor piece. You'll have to decide by measuring the overall height of the grouping, exactly where you are going to hang the dominate piece. This is the one I always start with and then make my measurements for the other pieces off of this one. Remember, whenever you hang a second piece to include the designated space between the two into your measurements, and so forth.

Another way to hang a grouping, which is particularly helpful if you have a large grouping made up of many individual pieces, is to acquire a long roll of paper that exceeds the outer dimensions of the grouping. If a single strip of the paper is not enough, cut off two strips and tape them together. You can also work with newspaper that is opened up and taped together to make a single sheet that is longer and wider than the outer dimensions of the grouping.

Lay the paper on the floor in front of the wall. Place each individual item on the paper in the exact place that you would like it to go. With a pencil, pen or marking pen, draw an outline of each individual piece on the paper. Mark on the paper where the center of the wire pulled taut is located. If the piece has a hanger of some sort on the back, like a saw-toothed hanger, mark its position on the paper.

Cut away the entire excess border surrounding the overall drawing of the grouping. You now have a template to work from that will make it very easy to locate all of your pieces. Then tape the paper to the wall in the exact position that you wish to hang the grouping. Make sure that you place the paper facing you and not facing the wall. Make sure that the drawing on the paper is level or your overall grouping will be higher on one end than the other. Attach your chosen hangers on the wall to match the markings on the paper. Tear the paper away and hang each piece, checking the spacing and level as you go. You should wind up with a spectacular grouping.

Hanging a Wall Grouping Over Stairs

As mentioned above, the Laser Beam tools can really be helpful when designing wall groupings over a staircase because you must work using the angle of the staircase. When choosing art for the staircase, they don't have to be small images, but since they will be viewed up close, this is an excellent place for images with small details and delicate lines or images that have a soft color palette. The landing is an ideal place to hang a very large image, assuming you have a wall sufficiently large enough to support it. It's also an excellent place to hang tapestries, antique rugs or quilts.

Lay all of your choices out on the floor first to make sure that they will be attractive if grouped together. The stronger the images or more active the image, the more "breathing space" they might require. Consider hanging these a little further apart than images that are very soft and "quiet".

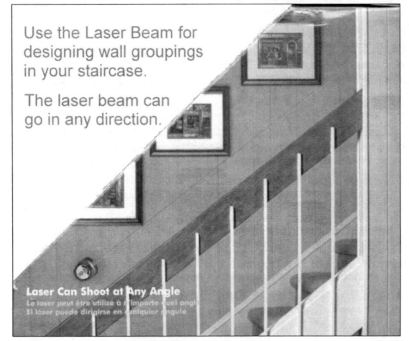

Use the Laser Beam for designing wall groupings in your staircase.

The laser beam can go in any direction.

Laser Can Shoot at Any Angle
Le laser peut être utilisé à n'importe quel angle
El láser puede dirigirse en cualquier ángulo

The procedure to hang a wall grouping over stairs is much like that which I have recommended for a normal wall. The difference and complexity will come in the form of the angle that steps create.

Ideally the angle of your grouping should be the same as the angle on the stairs. You can figure out this angle by measuring the distance from the ceiling to the floor at the base of the stairs, measuring the distance from the ceiling to the floor at the top of the stairs, and then measuring the distance from the bottom step to the top step. A good rule of thumb is to place the bottom of the images approximately 55" above the step where it will hang, that is if you are only doing one row of images. As I've stated earlier, five and 1/2 feet (66 inches) is considered the universal "eye level".

Once you have your measurements, draw it out on a piece of graph paper. After you draw the vertical lines the same corresponding distance from each other as the length of the stairs, you will arrive at the angle that the steps are creating.

Tape paper together until you have a sheet larger than the whole grouping you wish to hang. Decide where the center of the grouping shall be on the horizontal measurement. Place a diagonal line that is at the same angle as the stairs from one end of the paper to the other end. Arrange all of the pieces in the grouping off of this angled center line. Then follow the same directions mentioned in the section above, "Hanging a Wall Grouping" and you should discover that it's pretty easy to hang a wall grouping over stairs.

If you're more daring, cut a long piece of string or cord and lay on the floor at the approximate angle that the stairs have created. Start with your largest most dominate piece and place it on the floor above the string where you feel you're going to want it. Lay all of the other pieces on the floor, positioning them accordingly off of the first dominate piece.

Using your measuring tape, the push pins and your level, hang the first piece according to the standard instructions above for hanging a single image. Hang all subsequent pieces according to the layout you have created on the floor, keeping the spacing as equal as possible.

This is trickier and you may find yourself having to adjust hooks or nails as you go, but some of you may be just like me and would rather skip the paper template step. It just depends on how good you are at estimating things.

Be sure to hang every piece with adequate security. You don't want anything to fall down and get broken or hurt someone if it is accidentally brushed by someone going up or down the stairs. This is a really good place to use two hooks for each piece, or even consider installing them with security hardware so they cannot fall off if bumped by someone.

Security Hardware

Security hardware can be purchased from any local frame shop. There are different kinds. Some are for metal frames that are hollow on the back and others are for wooden frames that are solid wood. Security hardware usually consists of two hangers on top and one or two on the bottom. They are usually used in businesses where the business wants to keep the images securely hung so that they cannot fall or be stolen. Since security hardware is rarely used in the home, I'm not going to cover it, other than to say: Check with your local framer or hardware store. The typical security systems come with a security key for the installer to use, which you then leave for your clients so they can remove the art work when necessary in the future.

Be aware that images with security hardware are more time consuming to hang, require more precise measuring. They also leave larger holes in the wall because they require plastic screw anchors and screws (see picture in tool section). So determine first if you REALLY need security installation in that location, because it is rarely needed in a residential setting. If you decide you need it, I recommend making a paper template on the back of the framed image to help you get the precise measurements you're going to need -- or hire a professional.

Installing on Cement or Brick

Hanging art on cement blocks or brick is more complicated. I would advise hiring a local professional to install your pieces if you have difficult walls such as plaster, cement, stone or brick. The above instructions are for drywall walls, which are the most common.

Other Resources for Hanging Art

www.hanggups.com – New kind of hanging system that allows you to easily mark where the nail should go while you're holding your wire-hung artwork in place. It's called the

"HanggUp" (that's right, it has two "g's") and runs around $15.00 plus shipping. Pretty cool.

Innovative Design & Development Group – Oviedo, FL makes a clear triangular shaped hanger for artwork called "Wall Respector". It uses straight pins, yes, I said straight pins, to hang your pictures. Contact them for a retailer near you.

www.heavydutywallhanger.com – They sell a "no tools required" hanging hook. It's made especially for hollow core walls and paneling. It can be installed or removed in seconds. There's no need to find a wall stud. It's made of heavy gauge metal and will hold up to 150 lbs or as much as the wall itself will support.

Chapter Sixteen

Typical Furniture Arrangements That Work

Arranging furniture is really very simple to do if you just understand some basic concepts. Yes, the complexities enter into the equation in the form of the size and configuration of the room, but after years and years of working in this area, I have truly found that once you place the major seating element that the client owns in the right place, the rest of the room seems to naturally come together. That one single all important piece is usually a sofa. Get it in the right place and watch the room come together, no matter what the configuration. As long as a client has enough furniture and accessories for me to work with, I can take any space and any type of furniture (even if it doesn't particularly "go together") and make the space look smashing! And so can you.

So to help you further, I've put together a series of 33 furniture arrangements for you to study. Believe me, if you just learn the basic concepts involved in creating these types of arrangements, you'll be able to master any room, and any set of furnishings you come across. The answers all lie within these arrangements because they are just pretty typical of what you're going to run across out there. Sure the sizes and shapes change. But that's what makes it both fun and a challenge.

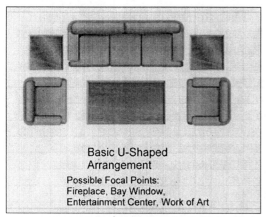

Basic U-Shaped
Arrangement
Possible Focal Points:
Fireplace, Bay Window,
Entertainment Center, Work of Art

Basic U-Shaped Arrangement

Here we have a very typical U-Shaped Furniture Arrangement. The anchor is the sofa, placed in the middle. It is flanked by two end tables. Two sofa chairs on each side create a symmetrical arrangement with the coffee table in the middle. Note that the space in front of the sofa and chairs is rectangular in shape. Use a rectangular or oval coffee table, not a square or round one. This keeps the correct proportions for the space. A sofa table can easily be added behind the sofa. This arrangement is very simple but for it to work effectively, you will want to have the end tables near a wall if there are lamps placed on them, for access to electrical outlets.

Basic L-Shaped Arrangement

A very typical arrangement, the L-shaped Arrangement is formed when one of the seating elements is shorter than the other. In

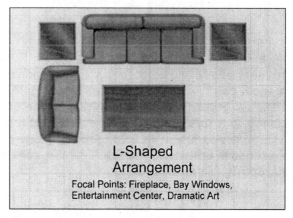

L-Shaped
Arrangement
Focal Points: Fireplace, Bay Windows,
Entertainment Center, Dramatic Art

this arrangement it's clear that the sofa is wider than the loveseat. This is an asymmetrical arrangement. You'll want to place the shorter section of the "L" so that there is easy access into the grouping from the direction most used. Again, if there are lamps placed on the two end tables, these tables should be near electrical outlets.

L-Shaped Sofa/Club Chair Arrangement

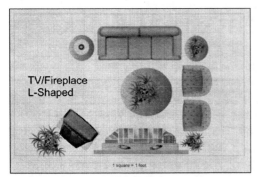

Any time a room has two strong functional uses, such as a fireplace and a TV, it is good to place the two "focal points" next to each other. Here we have an L-shaped arrangement comprised of the sofa, two end tables, two club chairs and a coffee table. In this arrangement, the space in front of the sofa and chairs starts to appear somewhat square, so this is why a large round table works well. But this arrangement could just as easily accommodate a rectangular or oval shaped coffee table. Notice that the TV is placed at an angle for easy viewing. An artificial tree or tall floor plant is placed behind the TV to hide the back from view. Be sure it is an artificial plant. A live plant would most likely die from the heat generated by the TV. In this arrangement, anyone seated any place can see the TV while enjoying a nice fire on a rainy day.

Flanked Fireplace Arrangement

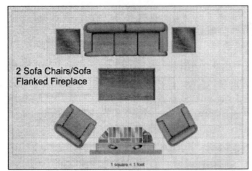

Another arrangement that is symmetrical and very open on each end is achieved by placing the sofa parallel to the fireplace. Two club chairs and the two positioned on each side of the fireplace, in this symmetrical theme. A coffee table is placed between. Be sure to keep the sofa back about 8-9 feet away from the hearth so that the arrangement remains cozy and intimate. If you place the sofa too far away from the focal point, you create "screaming distance" and the whole arrangement feels disjointed and uncomfortable. For greatest intimacy, place all seating fairly close to encourage easy conversation.

Basic H-Shaped Arrangement

Working with the perpendicular (90 degree) angles, a sofa and two sofa chairs face each other. However, both sets of seating elements are perpendicular to the focal point. A coffee table between them serves all seated persons. A plant is added to the sofa for balance, but this could also be a small table instead. Make sure you keep the arrangement fairly close so that there is unity and you don't inhibit conversation by creating "screaming distance".

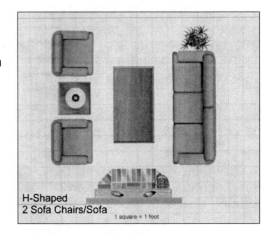

Parallel Sofa Arrangement

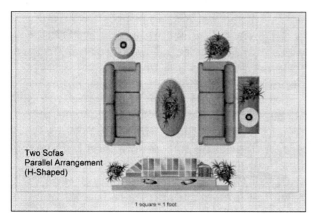

Two Sofas
Parallel Arrangement
(H-Shaped)

1 square = 1 foot

This is a variation from the one prior. Here we have two matching sofas that are placed facing each other, but perpendicular to the fireplace. An oval table fills the rectangular space between each sofa and serves all seated persons. But to create a little more interest and break from the symmetrical balance, two end tables are added. A lamp is placed on one and a plant on the other. A sofa table is added to the back of one of the sofas. Depending on the space in the room, there are even more elements that could be added, such as more plants, but you get the idea.

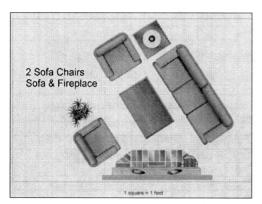

2 Sofa Chairs
Sofa & Fireplace

1 square = 1 foot

Angled L-Shape Arrangement

Now let's swing the seating around to an angle, roughly 45 degrees. Here we have another L-shaped Arrangement that is angled, using an end table and coffee table. A sofa chair is added to the mix next to the fireplace. The sofa chair should be placed completely parallel to the sofa for the best feeling. Add in more plants and accessories for a fabulous look.

Inverted V-Shape Arrangement

A more unusual arrangement is the Inverted V-Shaped Arrangement. This works well in a large room where there are two identical sofas. Place the sofas perpendicular to each other but where they are at a 45 degree angle to the fireplace. To change up the arrangement and break from the symmetry, put a sofa table behind one sofa and a group of floor plants behind the other one. A round or square coffee table will work nicely in this type arrangement. Just make sure there is sufficient room to navigate within the arrangement.

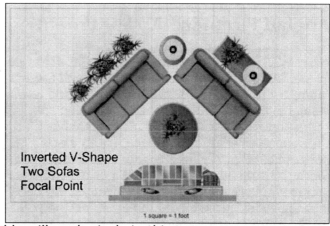

Inverted V-Shape
Two Sofas
Focal Point

1 square = 1 foot

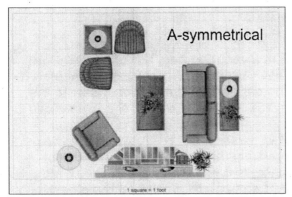

Asymmetrical Arrangement

I love asymmetrical arrangements because I think they are far more interesting because they are more unexpected and informal. In this arrangement we find a sofa placed perpendicular to the fireplace, a sofa chairs placed at an angle, and two club chairs with an end table in the opposite corner. The entire geometric shape of these elements is pretty square. A floor lamp has been added behind the sofa chair to bring some height to this side and a sofa table was added behind the sofa. The important concept here is to try to balance both sides of the room while keeping access easy. Notice that the entire arrangement remains intimate even though there is a lot going on.

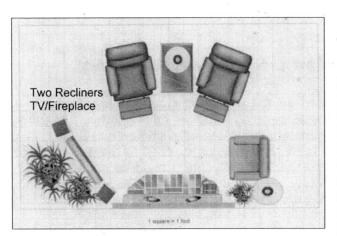

Two Recliners Arrangement

It's always more difficult to work with recliners than other types of seating because you have to allow plenty of space behind the recliner and in front of it. So recliners don't work too well if pushed up against a wall. Get them out into the open space. Pictured here are two matching recliners, a sofa chair and a flat screen TV near the fireplace. Trees behind the TV hide the wires and cables. A floor lamp helps to balance the other side (height wise) next to the sofa chair.

Angled Fireplace Arrangement

Whenever you have a fireplace placed at an angle in the room, usually in or near a corner of the room, try to place the sofa (or main seating element) parallel to the fireplace. Keeping the same angle is very important. If you cannot place the sofa parallel to the fireplace, try to place it perpendicular to the fireplace for the best feeling. Since the sofa is out in the middle of the room, and most likely the back of it is facing some entry into the room, place a sofa table behind the sofa to add more interest and height variations to this area and conceal the back of the sofa. The u-shaped arrangement includes an area rug to anchor the arrangement and repeat the angles of

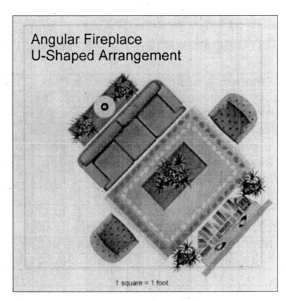

the furniture. Plants have been placed on both sides of the fireplace to fill these little empty corners and add more interest to the focal point of the room.

Angled Arrangement with Recliner

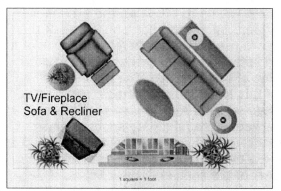

As mentioned earlier, when a room has a natural focal point, like a fireplace, and you also want to use the room to watch TV, then it's best to place the TV as close to the fireplace (or other natural focal point) as possible. This way you can arrange the furniture to face both the TV and the focal point at the same time. In this angular arrangement, notice that anyone sitting on the recliner or the sofa can see the TV easily and enjoy the fireplace at the same time. Always make sure, when placing a recliner in a room, that you have allowed enough space behind it and in front of it for someone to tilt the recliner backwards to the lowest position and raise the built in "ottoman" too. Notice there is a tree that has been placed behind the TV to hide the back from view. This, already mentioned, should be an artificial plant because a real one will not survive the heat from the TV.

Sectional L-Shaped Arrangement for TV

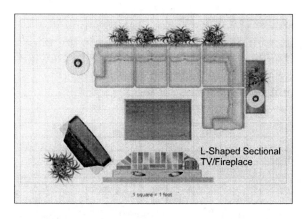

Sectionals can cause more problems because clients tend to want them to remain in the format they were purchased, so this can sometimes cause difficulty in creating an amazing arrangement. Here is your typical L-Shaped Sectional. A sofa table and floor plants have been added to the mix to bring height to the room and to hide the less attractive backs of the sectional. A wide screened TV is angled on the opposite side of the arrangement for balance and easy viewing.

Sectional L-Shaped Arrangement with Chair

In this arrangement, the wide screened TV has been removed and replaced by a club chair, floor lamp and tree. Depending on the client's possessions, just about any piece of furniture can be tucked in to the space next to the fireplace. If access to the arrangement is not needed next to

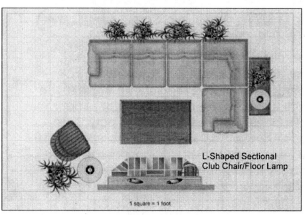

the fireplace, you could even close that off with an end table or more plants. Notice that the shape of the floor in front of the sectional is rectangular, so a rectangular coffee table still works well as in the previous example.

Split Sectional Arrangement

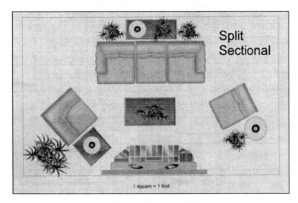

If a client is willing to break up the sectional, this is a more open arrangement. Three of the sections are used together to form the look of a standard sofa. Two other pieces are placed on either side of the fireplace. The geometric shape of this arrangement forms a half circle facing the fireplace. Add in plants, tables and lamps as needed to fill empty spots to finish off the arrangement. A sofa table with plants and a lamp add a unique touch to the back of the major part of the sectional. Easy access is maintained from two sides of the room.

TV and Fireplace Separated Arrangement

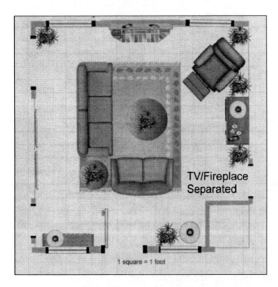

Sometimes clients place the TV further away from the natural focal point in the room, in this case the fireplace. Sometimes the configuration of the room or the size of the TV, the outlet for cable or other features in the room prevent the TV from being moved closer to the focal point. Here is an arrangement that makes it possible to enjoy the fireplace as well as the TV. The recliner is the only seating element that does not lend itself to viewing TV or enjoying the fireplace, so that makes this arrangement less than desirable.

Client Arranged Room with Bay Window at Top (before)

This client owned a very large area rug, a sofa and sofa chair. Not knowing any better, they placed the sofa up against the largest wall in the room (far right) and positioned the area rug accordingly. But notice how off balance the room is and how this arrangement totally ignores the room's natural focal point - the window with ledge. Look below for our solution to this room.

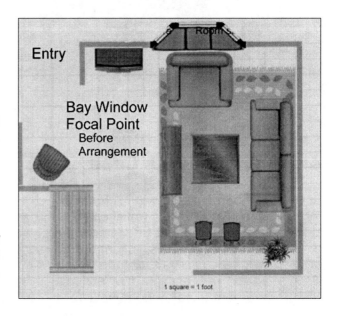

Bay Window Arrangement (After)

Bay Window
After Arrangement

1 square = 1 foot

The bay window is on the wall at the top of the picture. By swinging the large area rug perpendicularly and placing the sofa parallel to the large window, the room instantly took on an amazing quality and it instantly felt balanced as well. Two club chairs were brought in from another room and flank the window. By doing this the space in front of the sofa took on a more squared look which made it possible to keep the square table. Normally a square table does not work well with a longer sofa - the two are out of scale to each other. The sofa table is moved behind the sofa to add interest and height and hide the less attractive back of the sofa. Plants were brought in to fill in two corners.

Extra Wide Traffic Lane Arrangement

Extra Wide Traffic Lanes
TV/Fireplace as Focal Points

1 square = 1 foot

A member in this family suffered from cerebral palsy and needed the traffic lanes to be at least 4 feet wide. This is a little wider than normal. By dividing off this rather long room into two sections, using some of the seating and the TV at an angle, this arrangement worked out perfectly. The sofa remains parallel to the fireplace but is moved much closer than the homeowner had it. A sofa table and area rug were suggested as additions to the room. A small desk and chair from the kitchen were brought in to create an L-shaped arrangement in the lower corner with the tree and china cabinet. A club chair with art for the wall was placed on the opposite of the china cabinet for balance. This arrangement was exquisite.

Small Room Arrangement

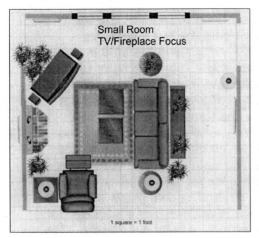

Small Room
TV/Fireplace Focus

1 square = 1 foot

For those clients who don't feel that comfortable with furniture placed at an angle, here is an arrangement idea for this small, square room. The longer coffee table has been exchanged for two smaller square tables. This makes navigation in and around the recliner easier. Again, traffic is encouraged to walk around the grouping rather than thru the middle of it. Artwork, plants or other pieces of furniture can also be brought in to complete the design of the room and placed in designated spots along the room's perimeter.

Angled Inverted V-Shaped Arrangement

Sometimes an architectural element, such as a heater, presents a unique problem (located at top of the room in front of window-filled wall). In this room, the three windows on wall would make a handsome focal point, were it not for the heater. But since there is a fireplace as well, the seating has been planned around the fireplace. In an Inverted V-shape, the sofa and sofa table are angled on one side of the fireplace and the two club chairs at the opposite corner. The square coffee table is usable because of the shape of the floor between the sofa and club chairs. Since the room is

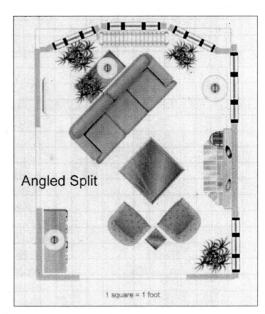

Angled Split

1 square = 1 foot

largely used for reading, a book shelf has been added to one corner to help balance the room. Artificial plants flank the heater. Don't try to use real plants this close to a heating unit.

Parallel Sofa
Loveseat

1 square = 1 foot

Sofa/Loveseat Parallel Arrangement

Taking a different approach, the sofa is placed perpendicular to the fireplace and the opposite, parallel side is filled by a loveseat. A large area rug which the client already owned has been kept to help anchor the grouping and tie things together for a very intimate, cozy and versatile arrangement. Lamps on both sides of the arrangement make reading easy. Two matching bookcases have been tucked into the uneven wall space flanking each side of the fireplace. A more formal arrangement, traffic is prevented from cutting through the middle of the arrangement.

Poor Client Arrangement Wall to Wall Fireplace (Before)

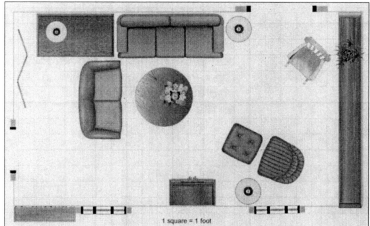

This room boasts a beautiful wall to wall fireplace on the far right wall. The client had created an L-Shaped Arrangement on a perpendicular wall, but the whole arrangement was too spacious and disjointed with little unity. When you are faced with a long room, it is often necessary to break the room into sections so that you can achieve unity, harmony, balance and intimacy. Below are several different arrangements of the same room. Notice how the room is first broken into 3 separate segments and then into 2 segments.

L-Shaped Arrangement with Wall to Wall Fireplace (After #1)

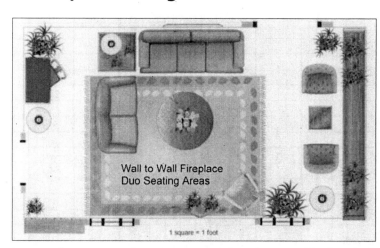

In this arrangement, the wall-to-wall fireplace lends itself to a separate setting for two. We placed two club chairs facing each other with a small table between. These are adjacent to the fireplace. This little seating arrangement is ideal for reading, for playing a game, or for having a late night romantic tea by a dreamy fire. A floor lamp and small tree are added to complete the look. The L-Shaped main seating arrangement is left where it was, however a large area rug has been added to help anchor this arrangement and clearly define three separate areas of the room. A small desk and chair, floor lamp and tree have been arranged against the far left wall for the 3rd section of the room. See how the room is now balanced, full and functional, all at the same time.

L-Shaped Arrangement with Wall to Wall Fireplace (After #2)

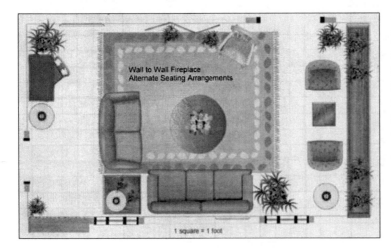

The L-Shaped Main Arrangement is kept but moved to the opposite wall. The rocker, folding screen and some plants are moved into the center section for balance. All else in the room remains the same as the prior arrangement.

Duo Purpose Arrangement with Wall to Wall Fireplace

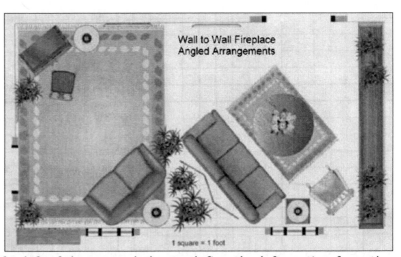

Now let's play around with some more unique angular arrangements, this time breaking the room into two nearly equal sections instead of one large one and two smaller ones. The sofa and love seat have been split apart, with one in one section of the room and the other one in another section. Plants, a floor lamp and the folding screen have been utilized nicely to divide the room further. Even the area rug, now pushed totally to the far left of the room, helps to define the left section from the right section. The desk and chair are now angled in one corner with the love seat for balance in the opposite "corner" of the section. On the far right, the rocker has been combined with the sofa to form an L-shaped arrangement that is angled against the wall-to-wall fireplace. In this arrangement, no one passing through the room will interfere with the visual enjoyment of the main seating arrangement.

Duo Purpose Arrangement 2

A variation of the prior arrangement, the two sections of the room remain clearly defined by the area rug, plants and folding screen. However, the main seating arrangement is now both parallel and perpendicular to the fireplace and the folding screen follows suit. Again there is no passing traffic that will interfere with

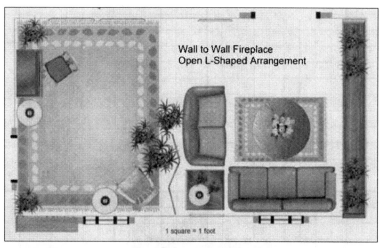

anything happening within the main seating arrangement. Strong, large art work is added to the walls that have no furniture to help balance the entire room and bring in extra personality and color.

TV in Corner Arrangement

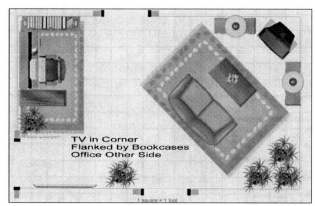

This client had a TV in the corner with no architectural element in the apartment to serve as a focal point. Two bookcases flank the TV with matching lamps. The area rug, sofa and coffee table were placed at a parallel angle with the TV. To balance that part of the room, we placed a grouping of plants in the other corner. A small home office was the perfect answer for the far left wall. It's perfectly fine to have two area rugs in the space so long as they coordinate in color. Area rugs are very important and a great help in anchoring a grouping and clearly defining the "island" in a room. They also help protect the flooring in areas where there is bound to be a lot of traffic wear.

Corner Entertainment Center Arrangement

This client had a very large, mostly square space that served as the family room and dining room. The doorway at the bottom led to the kitchen. The area also serves as a play area for a small child, whose bed for nap time had to be in the area where it could be viewed from the kitchen. A corner entertainment center provided the main function of the room. As you can see we arranged the room where anyone on either sofa could view the TV. Three floor futons were strategically placed in front of the TV for the younger kids to enjoy. The whole living room area is delineated by a very large area rug. Traffic coming in the front door (top wall) is forced to move to the right or left. When moving left toward the stairs they will not interfere with anyone watching TV. The child's toy chest is moved down near the dining room area for there is plenty of space there and the child can easily be monitored by the parent in the kitchen.

Client Arranged Master Bedroom (Before)

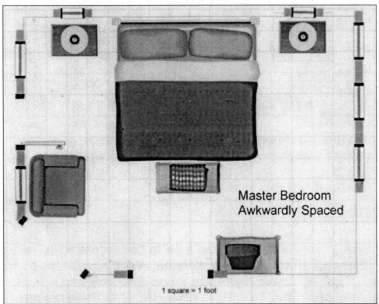

This master bedroom presented a bit of a challenge for the homeowner because the windows of the room are kind of in strange locations, breaking up the room quite a bit. The client placed the bed in the middle of the largest wall, not a bad location, however there was far too much space between the bed and the night tables making the arrangement feel disjointed. A large sofa chair was placed right at the entrance to the room blocking access a bit to the patio doors on the left wall. The small chest at the foot of the bed, normally an ideal location for a chest, was too short for the bed, making the king size bed look no larger than a full sized bed.

Master Bedroom Arrangement (After)

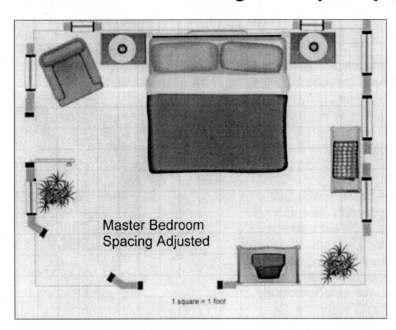

All that was needed here was a few adjustments. The bed was left in the center of the wall and the night stands moved closer so they are viewed as a grouping. The sofa chair was moved to the upper corner helping to fill the wall and opening up good access to the patio. The chest is moved from the foot of the bed to the far right wall where it helps to fill the space, balance the room and add interest to an otherwise bland set of windows. Instantly the bed appears wider. If you're going to put a chest or other piece of furniture at the foot of your bed, make sure it is the right scale. If it is not at least 2/3rds the width of the bed, it will be out of scale and will make the bed appear to be much narrower than it is.

Chapter Seventeen

Basic Home Staging Business

One of the most lucrative businesses you can conduct simultaneously to your redesign business is a home staging business, particularly in an economy that has an overabundance of homes on the market for sale. Home staging services were never more vital than now. This manual will teach you virtually everything you need to know to run a successful business in this field as well. Don't leave money on the table. Smart entrepreneurs do both businesses because they are so closely related and can be marketed together. To get your copy of **Home Staging for Profit,** visit this link at **http://decorate-redecorate.com/home-staging-training.html**.

Staging Luxurious Homes

One of the best overall marketing tactics is to concentrate a certain amount of your time and energy courting affluent homeowners and their agents. Why? Because they have the money to purchase your consultation services and your staging services. In addition to that, they are very busy people, usually concentrating more on making money than in selling their home, and they are naturally excellent candidates for a home staging service. I've written a one-of-a-kind tutorial that will teach you essentially everything you need to know to tap into this highly prized market and even specialize in staging wealthy homes. Get your copy now. Visit: **http://decorate-redecorate.com/staging-luxurious-homes.html**

Advanced Redesign

You have just completed the Basic Home Staging training. Home staging is really a fairly simple, straightforward business. It is simple to understand and simple to implement. But it will not be enough for some of you who are more enterprising and that really want to take your business to the next level. For you I have written the sequel called **Advanced Redesign**. It is 15 powerful chapters on how to take advantage of a number of other critical strategies and tactics to send your business onward and upward. You will not have time to implement all of these dynamite ideas and do them justice. No one does. But if you're really serious about building a highly profitable decorating business, then you should at least get the information on how you can acquire your copy of Advanced Redesign at **http://decorate-redecorate.com/advanced-redesign.html**.

Decor Secrets Revealed eBook

For top notch training in all of the necessary interior design principles and techniques of professional designers, consider getting my electronic book of 25 chapters devoted just to these specifics. The eBook has over 500 color photos. It is an easy, breezy read and will teach you a lot about furniture and accessory arrangement design, even if you've already had some design training. I've had full service designers with a 4-year degree tell me they learned from the training – or were reminded of concepts they had forgotten about. Please look on this as further investment in your success. Use this link to get your copy of **Decor Secrets Revealed** if you haven't done so already: **http://decorate-redecorate.com/decor.html**.

Arrange Your Stuff

Approaching furniture arrangement concepts from a slightly different angle, my 189 page soft cover (plastic comb binding) book of a wide range of sketched rooms, including the before sketch and then followed by anywhere from 1-4 sketches of how the room was and could have been arranged professionally. Lots of tips to help you immediately dissect any room and know how to solve it. Filled with the top and most common furniture arrangement configurations, you should find the answer to most rooms in these pages. Use this link to get your copy of **Arrange Your Stuff** if you haven't done so already: **http://decorate-redecorate.com/arrange-your-stuff.html**.

Wall Groupings! Secrets of Displaying Your Art and Photos

The replacement to my other book (Where There's a Wall – There's a Way), this book is filled with illustrations of wall grouping ideas. In addition to teaching you the secrets of how to properly arrange art in a wall grouping, it is loaded with photos of actual wall groupings from all over the country. You'll easily learn how to make sure the wall groupings you create for your clients are beautifully done – and you'll understand what makes a grouping work and what will make it impractical. The book also contains some templates for furniture and accessories. See the website for more details on this new book. You should really invest in this book too. You may read more about it here: **http://decorate-redecorate.com/book.html**.

Getting Paid!

Whenever you work for a client for more than a day, which is often the case in home staging, you run the risk of the client trying to get around paying you for your hard earned services and expenses. This can increase whenever the economy gets tight or slows down. People who otherwise would pay you start looking for ways to opt out. So you've got to protect yourself every step of the way. This manual will teach you how to make sure you always get paid. And should it ever become necessary to sue a client, it will teach you what steps to take to make sure you easily win your case. Check on our website for more details about this very valuable training at **http://decorate-redecorate.com/getting-paid.html**. Many people teach you how to start a business, but practically no one teaches you how to make sure you get paid. If you're doing home staging, this is a must have.

Dos and Don'ts in Home Staging and Redesign

In this exclusive, one-of-a-kind book, I show you 101 case studies (some of mine, but mostly those of some of my students). I show you the before picture and the after picture. I discuss what was wrong in the before picture, the way the client had arranged the room. Then I discuss what the stager or re-designer did to change and improve the room. I point out what worked, what didn't, or what else could have been done to help the client. Learning from the success and misses of others is an excellent way to reinforce what I teach, particularly from a design standpoint. Details on this book can be found at **http://decorate-redecorate.com/dos-and-donts-staging-redesign.html**

Home Staging in Tough Times

Once again, a one-of-a-kind, exclusive manual that teaches you how to grow your business, even in a difficult economic climate. There are many strategies you can utilize and many of them are free too. This advanced training is excellent for anyone, particularly if you are struggling or not happy with your income level. You'll find more details about this exclusive training at **http://decorate-redecorate.com/home-staging-in-tough-times.html**

Convert to a Course:

I also offer all-inclusive courses that cover in depth, not only the interior redesign business, but the related home staging business as well. If you purchased this tutorial and now wish to convert to one of our courses instead, please call us and we'll make arrangements to give you credit for your purchase. A conversion must be handled manually to give any credits. The choice is yours.

The best place to see a quick overview of everything currently available is at this link: **http://decorate-redecorate.com/home-staging-redesign.html**. It's a chart and you can easily see all of our "a la carte" components and compare them with our many course options.

Courses have been designed for those unique individuals who are really serious about building a career level business, want everything all at once, and want to save money in the process. It is not particularly a route I recommend for everyone, particularly if you're only interested in supplemental income or you would be too strapped economically as a result. That's why I offer plenty of options in an "a la carte" fashion so you can tailor your training and any additional products you might be interested in to your personal timing and resource limits.

But for those that can jump into a course, it makes the most sense. Duo certification is guaranteed with a Diamond Course and single certification is guaranteed with a Gold Course.

The Diamond Course includes design training, basic and advanced staging and redesign business training, multiple types of promotional aids to help you launch and promote your business, tools of the trade to help you actually do your projects, certification, directory listings, a members only site (with lifetime membership and no annual fees like others charge), VIP status on advice, and a bunch of other goodies thrown in.

Diamond Standard, Diamond Ruby and Platinum Courses - Our most comprehensive training programs, the Diamond Standard, Deluxe and Ruby Certification Courses give you all of the design training and business training you'll ever need (both basic and advanced), numerous sales aids, some management tools of the trade, double guaranteed certification, custom stationery to effective launch your business, brochure webpages or websites, double business listings in our directories and bonuses, but you get two businesses instead of just one. For details: **(Diamond Standard Course)** http://decorate-redecorate.com/diamond-redesign-training.html or **(Diamond Ruby Course)** http://decorate-redecorate.com/diamond-ruby-combo-course.html or **(Platinum Combo Course)** http://decorate-redecorate.com/platinum-combo-course.html .

Silver Combo Training - Get all of our two businesses plus redesign training in one easy package. This program does **not** include the "tools of the trade" – it is strictly training, but is all of our training eBooks and books for a packaged price for two businesses, not just one. For details: http://decorate-redecorate.com//silver-redesign-training.html

Visual Aids and Action Tools

Home Staging PowerPoint Presentation Slides and Script – Another great tool, this 65-Slide Presentation is great for use before real estate agents. It primarily promotes the services of a home stager, but ends with redesign as well. Comes with a script that you can edit for your own purposes. See **http://decorate-redecorate.com/home-enhancement.html**

Interior Redesign PowerPoint Presentation Slides and Script – Don't try to "tell" people what you do – "show" them with our exclusive 60-slide presentation. It comes with a full script which you can tailor to your situation. For use with Windows PC computers, whether or not you have PowerPoint. See **http://decorate-redecorate.com/redesign-slides.html**

Musical Slideshow Prospecting CDs – Don't try to "tell" people what you do – "show" them with our Before and After Musical Slideshow. It's the perfect way to turn a prospect into a client and makes it so much easier for you to sell the benefits of your

services. Available in sets of 3, 6 or 12. For the Home Staging Slideshow CDs, please visit **http://decorate-redecorate.com/staging-for-sellers.html**

For Interior Redesign Slideshows, visit: **http://decorate-redecorate.com/get-clients.html**

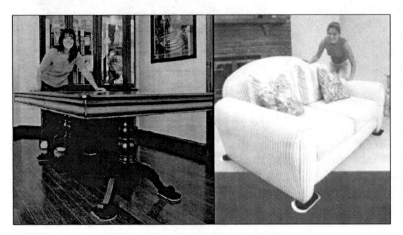

Furniture Sliders for Carpet or Hard Flooring – Don't hurt your back moving heavy furniture. Do it the easy, effortless way with furniture sliders. We have them for both carpeted floors and hard floors. See **http://decorate-redecorate.com/furniture-movers-carpet.html** or **http://decorate-redecorate.com/furniture-movers-hard-floors.html**

Decorating Organizer/Tote – It's hard enough to go shopping for your decorating projects and keep track of all your swatches and samples. We've got a very professional organizer/tote combination that makes it super easy. And you'll look classy too. This is a super organizing tool and I use mine all the time. See **http://decorate-redecorate.com/decorating-shopper.html**

Promotional Postcards, Folders, Business Cards – Use our colorful, professionally printed promotional postcards to get the word out about your services. Many styles to choose from. Cards are sold in sets. We have staging cards, redesign cards, staging & redesign cards, variety packs, quotation and presentation folders with matching letterhead and referral cards, and a quick start promo pack

See **http://decorate-redecorate.com/postcards.html**. See also **http://decorate-redecorate.com/quotation-folders.html** See also **http://decorate-redecorate.com/staging-promotional-paks.html**

The Home Staging for Yourself Checklist Guides are one of our most popular visual aids for helping you make money on every appointment. You'll always encounter people who want to do the staging themselves or who just refuse to hire professional stagers. With this 80-page Guide, you can fill it out for them so they can follow the instructions and stage their own home. You simply sell them the guide for a higher price than you paid. Since the list is so exhaustive, it will silently urge them to possibly hire you instead. For more details: **http://decorate-redecorate.com/home-staging-for-yourself.html**.

Furniture Arrangement Kit – One of the best overhead furniture arranging kits. You'll get around 1600 furniture decals to apply to special grid paper so you can create a bird's eye view of any room in your home or for a client. The furniture comes in multiple styles and sizes and all decals are reusable. See **http://decorate-redecorate.com/furniture-arrangements.html** For an Elevations Furniture Arranging Kit, visit **http://www.decorate-redecorate.com/furniture-elevations.html**

Additional Design Training Options

Flower Power – Whether you're decorating for a social event for your client or decorating your own home, knowing how to arrange flowers is a specialized talent you would do well to have. While we have some floral arranging training available in Advanced Redesign, you'll get the complete and thorough version in Flower Power: **http://floraldesigntraining.com**

Great Parties! Great Homes! – Learn how to decorate for parties and social functions, how to be the perfect hostess and how to be the perfect guest. **http://decorate-redecorate.com/planning-parties** Great training for learning how to effectively promote your business and acquire referrals. Since most business in staging and redesign happens through face-to-face relationships, being active socially is a crucial part of building your business.

Monthly Newsletters

Decorating Newsletter – While you're at it, sign up for our free Decorating Tips newsletter that comes out twice monthly. It's full of decorating tips and you'll be the first to learn about new products and get special discount coupons not available to the public. Just visit our home page and sign up. It's FREE. Decorate-Redecorate.Com

WorkingWomen911.Com – Get ongoing tips and free advice, specials and discounts for all working women at **http://workingwomen911.com**.

Certification for Those That Want It

Certified Staging or Redesign Specialist – Certification is not necessary for success, but some people really want that extra credibility so we have a private certification process for you. In addition to that, as more and more people enter the industry, and more and more claim to be certified by one entity or another, then it becomes more important to acquire a designation to

compete in the marketplace. We offer the most potent designation of anyone because you can't get ours by mere attendance at a seminar or by paying to gain access to someone's membership site. To earn our designation, you have to prove you have the knowledge and skills necessary to represent the industry professionally. That means you must pass an exam and submit a portfolio to be review. So when you tell someone how you achieved your designation, all others will pale in comparison, guaranteed. You may apply for single or double certification. Application fee. Apply here: **http://decorate-redecorate.com/certified-redesigner.html**

Contact Information

Barbara Jennings (Decorate-Redecorate.Com)
Publisher: Ahava Press
PO Box 2632, Costa Mesa, CA 92628-2632

Just as I have been teaching you to ask for referrals and testimonials, I myself would appreciate any positive testimonials and referrals you might share with me. Please write me and tell me what part of this manual has benefited you the most. If you are confused by any part, please let me know that too. support4@barbarajennings.com

And please tell your friends about **Decorate-Redecorate.Com**.

If They Can Do It – So Can You

"Your training has helped me tremendously, especially in gaining confidence in my abilities. It confirmed many things I already knew and did but taught me other things that I had yet to consider. I had only taken one course (elsewhere) when I received my first offer to stage a home. I felt I really needed more training and signed up for the Diamond Standard Course as soon as I could. - Nancy Grant"

"I did not have the financial ability to order the course(s) so instead chose to order each item a la carte, and study as I could afford to advance through the books and eBooks. The information provided has far more design information than APSD. I earned my CID last year while completing other courses, and can say that this training applies the principles of design in a practical and easily understood manner. . . . Although I have been staging investment properties for several years, I learned a great deal from this specific training. The instructions on art and accessories were great. The checklists offer a no-fail system that can be utilized immediately. - Bonnie Lou Wisniewski"

"I am very pleased with the information contained as well as the personal support and support materials available. I certainly feel a lot more confident about going out and offering my services than I did before I took the training. . . . I was impressed with the practicality of the information. I am sure the advice contained will save me from making many mistakes I might have made otherwise that could have cost me more than the price of the training. - Victoria Guillot"

"There are so many school and training out there. I only pick yours. First, you know what you are doing. You are the best. Second, you know business and marketing. Third, you have angel's heart that you really care of your students. You are not a sale people with lousy skill. I admire your talents, hard-working and providing the best service you can. I believe that I will learn a lot from you. Thanks for providing this great program for us, so we can have a new bright future with you holding our hands to do the right thing. - Li-An Chen"

"I began an interior design business a year and a half ago. I am specializing in window treatments. This book showed me how I can incorporate redesign into my current business. This book was wonderful in encouraging me to pursue ███████ services. I would suggest anyone looking to go into redesign to pick up a copy of ████ Diane McMillan"

"This is the best book on the subject of how to start a re███ ████ learned so much, I can't believe it. It has given me the confidence to launc███ ████ eople know what I can do. I am forever grateful for how generously ███ ████ xperience and wisdom. - Emma Scholl"

CPSIA information can
Printed in the USA
LVOW090016161012

303013LV00

.om

9 780961 802646